ARFID
AVOIDANT/RESTRICTIVE FOOD INTAKE DISORDER
A GUIDE FOR PARENTS AND CAREGIVERS

**FERNANDA DO VALLE
AND DR. BACY FLEITLICH-BILYK**

ISBN-13: 978-1-949868-90-6

Text Copyright © 2022 Fernanda do Valle and
Dr. Bacy Fleitlich-Bilyk.

Revision: Matthew Rinaldi

Published by Underline Publishing LLC
www.underlinepublishing.com

All rights reserved.

No part of this publication may be reproduced, distributed or transmitted in any form or by any means, or stored in a database or retrieval system, without the prior written permission of the publisher. The only exception is by a reviewer, who may quote short excerpts in a review.

DEDICATION

To my sons, Theo and Daniel, for teaching me that, just when we think we have all the answers, life goes and changes all the questions.
Fernanda do Valle

To all the families who believed in my work, giving me the opportunity to dedicate myself to helping them in my 25 years of clinical practice. I have followed my career for my patients and their family members, feeling recognized by the thing that most moves me: the smile that comes with recovery.
Dr. Bacy Fleitlich-Bilyk

To Daniela, my dear patient, who made me go back to school for this subject and keep believing that the treatment for ARFID, despite being a long and difficult journey, is worth it.
Manoela Figueiredo

I dedicate my words in this book to the families that are struggling and looking for help in dealing with the eating disorders of their children, who should be the source of nurturing, health, pleasure and socialization, but who are, at the moment, a source of suffering.
Maria Luiza Petty

INDEX

INTRODUCTION 11
PREFACE 17
PART I 21
    FOOD SELECTIVITY 23
    SO WHAT IS ARFID, AFTER ALL? 27
    FAMILY IN TREATMENT 39
PART II 47
    VENTING 49
    EARLY SIGNS 51
    FOOD INTRODUCTION 53
    IMPORTANT 57
    ADAPTATION AT SCHOOL 59
    THE ACCIDENT 61
    THE CHANGE 65
    PEDIATRICS IN THE US 71
    BEGINNING TREATMENT 75
    AT LONG LAST, THE DIAGNOSIS 83
    THE PATH 93
    PUTTING THE PUZZLE TOGETHER 101
    NEW DIRECTION 109
    STIGMA 135

ABOUT THE AUTHORS

FERNANDA DO VALLE

In 2009, after detecting, accepting and treating her eating disorder, she released her first book Eu, ele e a enfermeira... Na luta contra a anorexia. Since then, she has dedicated part of her time giving lectures, alerting young people and parents to the dangers of this disease, and pursued a career as a writer. She published five other titles, released by the same publisher: Dos desencontros ao encontro, Tesselas – A família mosaico, De:filha Para:pai, Crônicas de Frenelda – Aventuras na ter-ra do Tio Sam and Liberte-se: você nasceu para ser real, não perfeita. In 2020, her first book was translated into English, under the title Together... Our Fight Against Anorexia, released by Underline Publishing. The same year, she received the International Recognition of Brazilian Literature award from the International Academy of Brazilian Literature. She is currently studying psychology at Purdue University, with the objective of researching and learning more to help other children who, like her son (the inspiration for this book), have eating difficulties. Fernanda holds a degree in tourism from Pontifical Catholic University of Campinas and a degree in Photography from the New York Institute of Photography.

DR. BACY FLEITLICH-BILYK

Dr. Bacy Fleitlich-Bilyx holds a degree in medicine from the University of São Paulo Medical School as well as a master's and doctorate in child psychiatry from the Institute of Psychiatry, Kings College, University of London. Creator and coordinator of the Program for Treatment, Instruction and Study of Eating Disorders in Childhood and Adolescence (Protad) at the Institute of Psychiatry of the University of São Paulo Medical School (IPq-HCFMUSP) (2001-2015). She was also researcher at the National Institute of Developmental Psychiatry (INPD-FMUSP) (2011-2014) and head of the Infirmary for Children and Adolescents at the Institute of Psychiatry (IPq-HCFMUSP) (2013-2015). She currently provides clinical care in psychiatry and psychotherapy.

ABOUT THE CONTRIBUTORS

MANOELA FIGUEIREDO

Holding degrees in nutrition from Anhembi Morumbi University and journalism from Pontifical Catholic University of São Paulo and specialized training in eating disorders from Ambulim (IPq-F-MUSP), Manoela Figuiredo is coordinator of the Group Specializing in Nutrition, Eating Disorders and Obesity (Genta). She received instruction in Intuitive Eating from Evelyn Tribole and Wellness Coaching from Carevolution and Wellcoaches. A qualified instructor in Mindfulness-Based Eating Awareness Training (MB-EAT), she completed level 1 training in Mindful Eating-Conscious LivingTM (ME-CL1) with Jan Chozen Bays and Char Wilkins. She is the creator of the Behavioral Nutrition Institute and co-author of the books Nutrição comportamental and Comer com atenção plena.

MARIA LUIZA PETTY

    Maria Luiza Petty is a nutritionist with a degree from the School of Public Health (University of São Paulo), specialized training in Eating Disorders from Ambulim (IPq-FMUSP), a master's and doctorate in the Graduate Program in Nutrition from the Federal University of São Paulo. In addition, she has been a collaborator at Ambulim (IPq/HCFMUSP) since 2009, working in the group that cares for children with ARFID, a member of the Group Specialized in Nutrition, Eating Disorders and Obesity (Genta) and author of the book Lugar de criança é na cozinha.

INTRODUCTION

FERNANDA DO VALLE

Before sharing and, to a certain extent, exposing my son's difficulties eating, at a time when he's still a child, I thought a lot about whether I had this right —the right to decide for him.

Especially in a society in which, for many people, there is still so much stigma and judgment when it comes to topics that are largely misunderstood.

A society in which there are people who crucify mothers, fathers and caregivers, with no mercy or compassion, without measuring their words or their looks.

And this is precisely why we need to talk more about this, to break this taboo and prejudice against the unknown.

The first time I heard of Avoidant/Restrictive Food Intake Disorder (ARFID) was in late 2018, when my son Theo, seven at the time, was diagnosed with it in the United States.

After researching, reading and studying the subject, I discovered that it is quite possible that my own eating disorder started out as ARFID during my childhood.

And this was another reason that made me bring something so private about my son's life out into the open.

I believe that, if my parents had known at the time what eating so selectively could be and what it might trigger, they would have sought help and much of the suffering in my life could have possibly been avoided.

Today, when I reread my book Together - Our Fight Against Anorexia, in which I recount the process of overcoming my disease, I clearly identify some aspects that are quite characteristic of ARFID when describing my dietary restriction. And even after having overcome my eating disorder, I still have difficulties with the smell and texture of some foods, symptoms that may be well fall under the diagnosis of ARFID.

Having been an extremely selective child, I was labeled a "picky eater." I developed anorexia nervosa in adulthood and this selectivity may have contributed to the evolution of my case.

During my childhood, I had no problem eating what I liked, but it was a very short list which excluded entire food groups. And I had lots of "demands."

My palate has always been very sensitive and, even I was going to have a glass of milk, the milk had to be a specific brand. The same thing went for chocolate milk. The milk had to be very cold, too. Any variation on one of these three factors and I couldn't drink it.

So of course I was known as the "fussy one" in the family.

Unfortunately, even today, it's hard to find much information and there are very few professionals prepared and trained to deal with this diagnosis.

I had to travel a long road with my son before finding a doctor who knew what ARFID was.

In this process of seeking help, I had to listen to plenty of hard truths, or rather "half truths."

I even heard from renowned pediatricians, and I'm talking about more than one, pediatricians whom I paid (expensive) private consultations, that I was not a good model of mother for my son and that he needed to go hungry to appreciate what was on the table.

Some doctors suggested that he was pampered, spoiled and that he was just trying to get attention.

I heard from other people that if he'd been born in Africa, he would eat whatever he got on his plate. I also heard that if he were poor, he wouldn't be so "picky." A "friend" implied that he was forever on a diet, as if I had imposed this on him, forbidding him to eat certain things.

People told me it was my fault because I had an eating disorder. And, of course, that really got to me and I believed it for many years.

And this among so many other outrages, which made me feel even guiltier than a mother usually feels whenever something isn't right with her child. I think when we become mothers, the word "guilt" is automatically incorporated into our last names. In the maternity ward, I became Fernanda Guilt do Valle. I didn't need any outsiders pointing their fingers at me to feel guilty. I naturally felt guilty already. But all the judgments, looks and sentences that I received further enhanced this feeling.

The first time I spoke publicly about ARFID was on Instagram. Before I did a live stream to talk about Theo's difficulties with food, I asked my followers if any of them knew about the subject. The vast majority responded that they had never heard of this eating disorder.

The scariest thing is that many of the people who answered that they were unaware of ARFID were healthcare professionals.

After the live stream, I received hundreds of messages from mothers who identified with what I had just shared. I have also received an incredible amount of reports from adults who went a lifetime with no diagnosis, without feeling understood and welcomed, and only recently found out they had ARFID.

Many of the adults had even been incorrectly treated for anorexia, bringing more emotional damage to their lives.

The curious thing is that many of the mothers of children with ARFID, or adults with ARFID, didn't learn of this eating disorder from their doctors.

These people found about ARFID on their own by researching and trying to understand what was happening to their children, or themselves—from a book, a news article or a documentary. And only then, after bringing this diagnosis up for discussion with a professional did they officially receive the "title."

After the live stream in which I presented Theo's case, I invited Dr. Bacy Fleitlich-Bilyk, co-author of this book, to talk more about the subject, but from a doctor's perspective.

At the end of the interview, I asked her for recommendations of Portuguese literature on ARFID. And that was when we came to the unfortunate conclusion: there is virtually nothing about ARFID available in the publishing market.

With each passing day, I continued to receive more and more messages, with questions about ARFID, with requests for help and treatment recommendations.

After interviewing Dr. Bacy, I also interviewed Manoela Figueiredo and Maria Luiza Petty, the two nutritionists who contributed to this book, on Instagram.

And it was in this context that this work was born. Realizing the shortage of information on this subject, which is still largely unknown and not talked about even in the healthcare field, the four of us came together to write this book.

Our very own fantastic four, a doctor and two nutritionists, all of three with exceptional professional brilliance, bringing their technical knowledge, and a mother who, though not yet an expert (I began studying for my degree in psychology here in the US), presents the other side, the experience of living with a child who has difficulty eating every day.

This book is not a substitute for professional help.

This book is not the only way. In fact, we're going to show you here that there isn't just one way.

This book is a light to help you find your path.

And the good news is you don't have to walk it alone.

We're here with you.

I leave you now with the words of the experts, who will provide clarifications on ARFID in an objective, transparent manner, but with great skill and mastery.

I'll be back later to talk about the challenges, the conflicts, and also the accomplishments of this journey with my little one.

Until then.
Warmly,
Fernanda

PREFACE

DR. BACY FLEITLICH-BILYK

You might be asking yourself why we need another book on eating problems. The answer is simple: we're going to address a specific subject that has been presenting innovations, not only in its diagnostic manual, but also in the treatments currently available.

We will provide parents and caregivers the latest information that we have found in scientific literature and clinical treatments, rendered faithfully, but in adapted language that is accessible to readers.

Up until 2013, the diagnostic classification included: Anorexia Nervosa (AN), Bulimia Nervosa (BN) and Eating Disorders Not Otherwise Specified (EDNOS). This classification was incomplete and insufficient for evaluating and diagnosing all patients and it often did not lead to specific diagnoses and appropriate treatments.

People working in the field ended up using informal classifications to lead patients to the best approach to be used, but these classifications weren't standardized at the various centers specialized in eating disorders.

In addition to the previously mentioned diagnoses (AN, BN, EDNOS), EDNOS functioned as an umbrella term that covered several groups of patients with different symptoms. Some nomenclatures emerged in England (Lask, 2000) to classify these groups: Food Avoidant Emotional Eating Disorder, Food Refusal, Comprehensive Refusal, Cibophobia, Functional Dysphagia, Sensory Food Aversion, Selective Eating Disorder and Restrictive

Eating Disorder. But it's very important to remember that these diagnoses were never given an official translation, being that this terminology was not listed in the Diagnostic and Statistical Manual of Mental Disorders, which at that time, before 2013, was in its fourth revised version (DSM-IV-TR).

So healthcare professionals like myself did our work, evaluating the patients clinically, diagnosing them according to what was most appropriate, considering the symptoms presented by the child and/or adult.

ARFID appeared for the first time in the new classification of DSM-5 (APA, 2013), which relied on the help of several eating disorder specialists so that the diagnoses categorized as Eating Disorders Not Otherwise Specified could be expanded and defined, in order to help clinicians and researchers to test the best treatments.

This change was also made to expand the symptoms and to include adults who were left out of the previous diagnosis, known to as Feeding Disorder of Infancy or Early Childhood.

And this is the story behind the "birth" of Avoidant/Restrictive Food Intake Disorder (ARFID), which is the theme of this book.

Since this classification is still very recent, we did not find many studies, care protocols, articles and literature on ARFID.. And this is why this book is so important, as it provides people with more information on the subject.

The content was structured in order to accurately address the questions we often get from parents and caregivers.

They include questions that many healthcare professionals themselves are sometimes unable to answer: What is ARFID? Who can develop it? Can it be treated? Is there a cure?

We will bring all this information based on science, the result of much study and experience, both professional and personal, and we will do so with the human warmth and care that our readers deserve.

We will offer hope and comfort to alleviate the uncertainties and anguish of those who live with people who suffer from feeding difficulties.

Warm regards,
Dr. Bacy

PART I

FOOD SELECTIVITY:
UP TO WHAT POINT IS IT NORMAL?

MANOELA FIGUEIREDO
MARIA LUIZA PETTY

Throughout a child's nutritional development there are several situations that create obstacles in the path of food acceptance. It's relatively common for the transition from breastfeeding to solid food to not go smoothly, raising concerns and tensions between the caregiver and the baby, for instance. Another frequent occurrence, which can first appear and intensify between age two and five, is food neophobia, namely the fear of trying new foods. This is a natural mechanism that has the function of protecting the child who, at this age, already has more autonomy, but is still cognitively immature and may end up trying to eat something inedible.

Another aspect that hinders food acceptance are innate aversions to certain flavors, such as sourness and bitterness. Foods with sour flavors are typically not rich in energy and can also be rotten—have you ever accidentally tried rice that was forgotten in the fridge for several days? In addition, many poisonous plants, for example, have a bitter taste. So, our bodies wisely create a natural resistance to foods that have these flavors in order to protect us, but, at the same time, this makes it difficult for us to like foods that are safe and essential for our health, such as fruits and vegetables, foods most often rejected by children.

These are some factors that make it so that food acceptance must be learned, which can take some time and may be influenced by the way this process is handled by caregivers.

Teaching children to like a variety of foods is not always an easy task. If food neophobia is a factor, it is essential for the child to have frequent contact with and observe other people eating certain foods to feel safe when doing so themselves. This means that if parents are not available or cannot model consumption, it may be more difficult for children to enjoy certain foods. Also, if, at the first sign of refusal, the caregiver substitutes what was rejected with a palatable, easily acceptable food, it's possible that there is no process of nutritional learning. On the other hand, if there is strong insistence that the child eats, this generates conflicts and even causes crying and vomiting, it is possible that the child associates the moment of eating with something stressful, making food acceptance even more difficult.

Probably, not coincidentally, about 25% of children have some degree of food selectivity throughout childhood. For most of them, however, this event will be natural, something that passes and causes them no harm.

Other factors can also lead to eating difficulties that impact the variety and/or quantity of what someone eats. Problems with chewing, swallowing and/or digestion of foods can generate discomfort that possibly creates memories (though perhaps unconscious ones) that eating certain, or many foods, is not pleasurable. So, even though children can't chew fibrous foods very well, for example, don't know how to describe that this is the problem, they will start to avoid them, having the feeling that they don't like anything that is even remotely similar to the thing they once ate that brought an unpleasant sensation to their mouth.

In order to eat, we need to develop a number of skills and competencies, including knowing how to chew. But in addition to this mechanical component, for us to feel safe and comfortable and to take pleasure in food it is essential for us to have the ability to process and tolerate all the sensory stimuli that it provokes.

Fernanda will explore these issues further in the second part of the book, but right now it's important for you to understand that, when we eat, we're subjected to various stimuli, such as smell, appearance, textures, temperature, flavor, etc., and all at the same time. These stimuli need to be quickly recognized by our nervous system and translated so that we can identify what we're putting in our mouth.

For most people, this system of recognition, translation and integration of sensory stimuli will mature every day, from birth, with the experiences we have.

But, unfortunately, some children exhibit a flaw in this maturation process and many problems can arise from that, since few things are as sensorial as food, don't you agree?

In these situations, several flavors, aromas and textures become extremely bothersome and disturbing, capable of generating feelings of disgust, fear and an avoidance of foods as a consequence.

To know if this is one of the causes of food selectivity, it is important to note that, normally, when an individual fails to process and integrate sensory stimuli, they usually have other difficulties in addition to food. It is common for the child (or adult) to not like stepping on grass or sand, to not be able to stand having dirt anywhere on their body, to be bothered by often imperceptible noises or scents that don't affect most people, to be irritated by bright light, etc. In these cases, it's also very common for feeding difficulties to start early on, often already during breastfeeding or food introduction.

It's very important to understand that, in situations in which there is any kind of discomfort associated with eating, be it mechanical, sensory or emotional, parents can present the food on countless occasions, eat it in front of the child, take them to the kitchen, make a clown face with the food, teach them about all the vitamins and minerals, and, still, the chances of success are small. In these situations and when the refusal is especially prolonged, it's time to seek help from professionals, preferably specialists.

Food refusal can not only cause harm to a child's health, but it can also compromise their social and emotional relationships. And though this may not be happening now, because today your child is fully adapted at home, one day he or she will grow up and have problems eating at parties, restaurants, friends' homes and while traveling.

So, to summarize, there are factors that hinder food acceptance in childhood and which can lead to increased selectivity. However, depending on how this phase is handled, for most children, these difficulties will be overcome and not have an impact on their lives. In other cases (which are the minority), a combination of additional factors, such as organic, sensory or temperamental problems, etc., can make selectivity and food refusal even more serious, severely impacting their lives.

In these, more serious cases, it is essential that caregivers seek specialized help as soon as possible so that they can start treatment for the child, but also to receive guidance on how to do it at home, as the family has a crucial role in the treatment.

SO WHAT IS ARFID, AFTER ALL?
(AVOIDANT/RESTRICTIVE FOOD INTAKE DISORDER)

DR. BACY FLEITLICH-BILYK

The term ARFID is unknown to many people, because, as mentioned in the preface, Avoidant/Restrictive Food Intake Disorder only officially came into existence as a diagnosis in 2013. However, we know from clinical experience that the eating difficulties that fall under this term are situations that have long existed and, therefore, we can say that it is a new old diagnosis.

It's important to emphasize that those with ARFID are not simply "uptight" and certainly not "picky eaters" just "looking for attention" from others.

Many parents and caregivers, as Fernanda recounted in the introduction to this book, describe being subjected to numerous inappropriate comments, including from professionals to whom they had turned for help.

Although ARFID typically affects children and adolescents, this disorder also manifests in adults, involving the same diagnostic criteria presented in this chapter. Often the clinical damage can be even greater, because adults with ARFID were most likely children whose conditions were never treated, and the habits of restriction and/or selectivity lasted for many years. The sooner the intervention, the better.

It's necessary to understand that individuals with ARFID show a lack of interest in food, often fear, dread, aversion, sometimes even revulsion at the sight of food. They may even experience a lack of appetite. These people don't stop eating because they want to lose weight. Unlike cases of anorexia nervosa, with ARFID, there is no concern with weight and/or obsession with body shape.

There is also anxiety and enormous difficulty when trying new foods and very strong resistance in agreeing to try anything "unknown."

These people can only eat what they consider to be safe foods, ones that bring them comfort and a sense of protection.

What each person considers safe varies from case to case, but what is common among all people with ARFID is that this list of foods is very selective and restricted, often causing a deficit in energy and nutrition for the individual, which can lead to serious damage to their physical health. These people will often only eat a few specific food textures and in very small amounts, and it can also take them a long time to finish a meal.

Those who have ARFID also end up suffering damage to their social lives, due to the difficulty they have among friends and family at events that involve food.

In addition to the physical harm, ARFID brings emotional damage, generating stress and suffering for the individual, as well as the entire family. This is why it's very important for the whole family to receive instruction, support and even therapy in order to learn how to deal with the tensions and disagreements that arise when they have someone with ARFID in their house. In the next chapter, the nutritionists will address the family's role in treatment.

As with any other eating disorder, there is no single reason or explanation that accounts for why a person has ARFID. Studies indicate that the cause is an accumulation of factors that are genetic, social, cultural and psychological in character, making it extremely complex.

ARFID can also be triggered after a bad or traumatic experience with food—a near-choking incident, for example. Or it can also happen as a result of a food allergy, after the individual has an allergic reaction from eating something.

These are triggers that enhance the development of the disorder, but not necessarily everyone who experiences a food-related trauma will have an eating difficulty afterwards.

One person may have a near-choking incident and develop ARFID while another may experience a similar situation without doing so.

Therefore, we need to be cautious of generalizing. Each case requires its own individual evaluation.

Speaking of generalization, it is very important for us to make an observation here. When reading about ARFID, several articles state that one of the determining factors for the diagnosis is low weight. However, it is important to make it clear that this is not a condition capable of determining that a child or an adult has ARFID (by children, we mean teenagers too).

In my clinical work, I have met many children with ARFID to whom this criterion did not apply. I've also known adults in the same situation.

I have treated cases of people with low weight, some with extremely low weight, but I also saw cases of people who would be considered healthy if evaluated only according to this parameter. In fact, ARFID can also occur in overweight or obese children, although these cases are rarer.

A diagnosis based on weight alone can greatly delay the process of seeking appropriate treatment.

It's necessary, above all, to evaluate the restricted (limited in quantity) and selective (limited in variety) eating behaviors and the impacts and harms that these limitations can bring.

It's also very important to exclude other diagnoses that include symptoms similar to those previously described, but associated with another medical condition, which may also present major food refusal, such as gastroesophageal reflux, food allergies, motor and oral impairments, dental problems and adenoid hypertrophy, among other causes. Some causes are visible and others aren't. This is why a comprehensive evaluation is needed to rule out whatever discomfort the person might be feeling, causing them to associate the act of eating with something that causes pain.

The diagnosis of ARFID is also disregarded when a person doesn't eat due to lack of available food and/or cultural issues.

According to the studies, there are three subtypes of ARFID:

- SELECTIVE EATING: selectivity may be associated with sensory issues. A person is unable to eat if he or she smells the food, sees its appearance, feels the texture or tastes the flavor. Many times they can't even try or get close to certain foods, due to all of these issues involved;
- RESTRICTIVE EATING: there is an indifference to food, a disinterest in food. Even when they do eat, they do so in very small portions, and they might have no appetite at all;
- REFUSAL TO EAT OUT OF FEAR OF ADVERSE EFFECTS: when there is a previous traumatic physical and/or emotional experience related to the act of eating, such as a near-choking, food poisoning or food allergy, generating a strong fear of eating in the individual.

It is not uncommon to find children and adults who show characteristics of the three subtypes.

SELECTIVE EATING

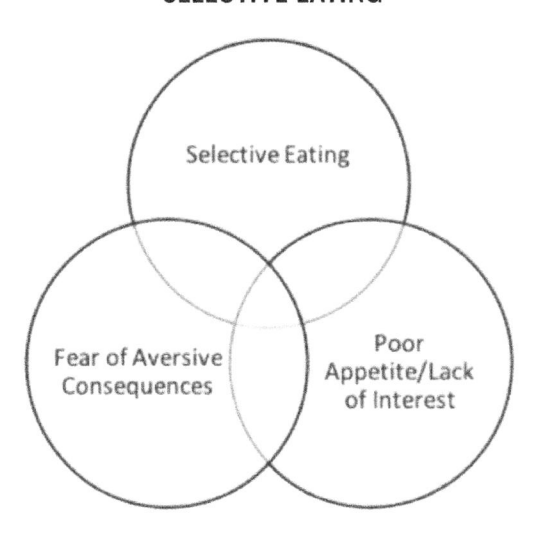

Venn diagram with three overlapping circles labeled: Selective Eating, Fear of Aversive Consequences, Poor Appetite/Lack of Interest

EATING DISORDERS CATALOGUE

As previously described by Manoela and Maria Luiza in the chapter on food selectivity, when selectivity is associated with sensory issues, it's essential to investigate whether sensory sensitivity is linked to eating alone. It's possible that the child presents other major sensory difficulties, which may be related to Sensory Processing Disorder. This disorder interferes with the way the brain receives, interprets and responds to the information that arrives through sensory stimuli: hearing, vision, taste, touch and smell—and we also have the proprioceptive and vestibular systems, responsible for the ability to recognize and process movements and changes in the body's position in space.

Therefore, once again, I emphasize the importance of evaluating the child in an integrated manner. When you have a sensory processing disorder, there is a deficit in the neurological process that organizes the sensations of the body and this may be reflected in the child's eating difficulties, and other difficulties that are not always visible. We may think that a child is messy, lazy, fearful, with an explosive temper, when, in fact, these are behaviors in response to the sensory difficulties that they face.

In the second part of the book, you will get more details on this subject and accompany a real case of the difficulties associated with Sensory Processing Disorder.

CLINICAL RISKS

In general, the restriction or avoidance of food can lead to serious clinical consequences:

- weight issues and height-growth problems;
- changes in sleep;
- weakness and dizziness;
- absence of menstruation (in adolescent girls or women);
- muscle weakness;
- constant sensation of coldness;
- dryness of the skin;
- weakness in nails and hair;
- constipation and abdominal pains;
- nutritional deficiencies;
- dependence on feeding tube or dietary supplements;
- interference with the normal functioning of daily activities.

It is noteworthy that people who have ARFID may not have all these consequences at the same time. They may not even have any clinical consequences. The longer they go without proper food, the worse the damage. But it isn't necessary to have a clinical injury to be diagnosed with ARFID.

Food provides us with energy for all sorts of everyday activities, such as sleeping, keeping warm, resting and staying alive. Our brain consumes energy, just like all the other organs in our body. When we talk about spending energy, it's the same thing as saying spending calories. This expense depends on our everyday activities. In addition to the energy needed to carry out their activities, children and adolescents also need calories to grow. And when there is a restriction and/or avoidance, it is possible that this child/adolescent will cease to develop properly.

In addition to physical development, there is also intellectual development. And a diet with nutritional deficiencies can result in major harm to the brain. It can give way to difficulty concentrating, in turn delaying learning. In the case of adults, it may have a negative impact on work. In addition, children and adults can experience many disadvantages in terms of their social lives, as they may end up isolating themselves due to the embarrassment of not being able to socialize in situations that involve food. Parents also fear that their child will feel unwell from spending hours without eating and, as a result, they often don't give them permission to participate in social activities, such as school field trips or friends' parties.

Nutritional deficiencies vary according to the eating profile of each individual who suffers from ARFID. The most common deficiencies are:

- iron (anemia);
- calcium and vitamin D (osteopenia);
- vitamin A (skin and eye problems);
- vitamin C (low immunity).

In addition to those listed above, other conditions commonly found in the blood tests of ARFID patients include low potassium, variation in the thyroid and other hormones, etc. In cases of low weight, there can also be a decrease in heart rate, which is a manner by which the body can save energy.

This issue of nutritional deficiencies is very well addressed in a famous example of a New Zealand teenage with an extreme case of ARFID, presented in a documentary produced by TVF International, The Truth About Fussy Eaters. He lost his vision due to a severe deficiency of vitamins in his body, resulting from malnutrition. Starting from when he was little, his mother spent years complaining of his "food selectivity" to doctors, who told her it was a phase, that it would pass, that he would learn to eat at school, etc. He had always been within the growth curve in terms of height and weight and, for many years, had a healthy appearance, so there was no concern from professionals. He only ate what foods from what we call the "Beige Diet" or "Soft White Foods." It's quite common that there is a pattern of textures, colors or shapes in the foods eaten by people with ARFID. In his case, he would only eat french fries and chicken nuggets. If he had received the appropriate treatment during his childhood, the damage certainly could have been avoided.

In more severe cases of ARFID, feeding tubes and the use of dietary supplements may be necessary. In general, in cases where feeding tubes are used, the procedure is thoroughly discussed among staff members, family members and caregivers. The use of feeding tubes in children or adults with major nutritional refusal, both in the quantity and variety of foods, will not effectively treat ARFID, but it can be extremely necessary if the insufficient supply of calories and nutrients places the individual's life in danger.

If a feeding tube is used, it is recommended that oral feeding continue to be offered and that a plan be made in order for the feeding tube to be removed as soon as possible.

ARFID can also occur in conjunction with other psychiatric diagnoses, such as children and adults who are on the autism spectrum. And here the feeding difficulty is closely associated with sensory issues, which will be presented in the second part of this book. Individuals with ARFID and sensory difficulties may also have other diagnoses such as Attention Deficit Hyperactivity Disorder (ADHD), Anxiety Disorder or Obsessive Compulsive Disorder (OCD).

Though ARFID is commonly diagnosed in children with autism, it's important to remember that children with typical development can also present the diagnosis.

TREATMENT

Since the diagnosis of ARFID is still very recent, there are few studies available on the efficacy of treatment. What we do know now is that approaches with behavioral intervention are generally the most recommended. However, considering the various symptoms and all the complexity that the diagnosis can present, a standardization that utilizes just one treatment protocol is not adequate.

The most commonly used approaches are Family-Based Therapy adapted for ARFID, Cognitive-Behavior Therapy and Behavior Analysis. In cases which include sensory issues, the SOS Approach and other such concepts are most often recommended, as Fernanda will thoroughly explain in the second part of the book.

But for those of you who are mothers, fathers or caregivers, the important thing is to get help from an interdisciplinary team, which will conduct an extensive, detailed evaluation of all your child's difficulties, also investigating other areas of functioning, in addition to food.

The result of this interdisciplinary assessment will be the basis for directing the combination of approaches to be used in treatment.

For some patients, the main symptom is fear, a phobia of ingesting food, while, for others, it is restriction, selectivity and feeding difficulties directly associated with sensory difficulties. And, as previously stated, it's even possible to find more than one major symptom in the same individual.

Therefore, the approaches are always synergistic. It's important to define an initial approach, but more important than this is to adjust, adapt and combine therapeutic techniques for each case, since each case is particular, due to all of the previously described complexity.

In any case, it is recognized that the approach should be interdisciplinary, involving nutritionists, psychologists, physicians and, in some cases, occupational therapists and speech therapists. And here it doesn't matter whether the treatment is being conducted at a specialized center that treats eating difficulties or it is an individualized treatment at a private practice. An interdisciplinary team is fundamental to the treatment's success.

Regardless of which line is chosen, it's very important that psycho-educational work is done with parents and caregivers so that, from the beginning, everyone is aware of the difficulties identified and in agreement and harmony with the agreements made between the team and family, for the treatment's progress.

Everything that is determined should always be explained very clearly to the parents, and the children, depending on their age, in language they understand, must be involved in this process too.

Getting a diagnosis won't cure anyone, but it's a very important starting point for proper treatment. Treatment time depends on the evolution and response of each person. It's a process that can be long and grueling, but certainly with many achievements and positive advances.

In the case of adults, the difficulties in socializing and maintaining relationships, because of all the limitations and consequences involved in ARFID previously mentioned, can be strong motivators in the search for help and treatment.

IS THERE A CURE FOR ARFID?

As with many cases in medicine, healing is directly related to the expectation of patients, family members and caregivers, as well as the actual professionals in the team.

Treatment goals should be discussed so that everyone can come to an agreement to work together.

The sooner the diagnosis is made and the treatment started, the better the prognosis and the greater the chances of being cured.

But what does it mean to be cured?

One family's idea of being cured may be quite different from for another's.

One family might expect their child to eat everything and a lot of it, whereas, for another family, the main goal may be for their child to eat enough food, in variety and quantity, to ensure proper growth, without having to rely on supplements.

Perhaps the cure doesn't mean that the child (or adult) will accept all the foods offered, but that parents and all those involved will be satisfied with the progress achieved.

Diminishing the suffering and minimizing the harm to the child, whether physical and/or emotional, are very important steps and should be seen as part of the cure.

A happy family, sharing the moments of mealtime together, without the stress and anxiety associated with the eating disorder, is, without a doubt, the cure too.

FAMILY IN TREATMENT

MANOELA FIGUEIREDO
MARIA LUIZA PETTY

Having a child with eating difficulties generates angst, uncertainty, suffering and often a sense of failure on the part of the family, especially for mothers, who ask themselves what they have done wrong or failed to do for their children, as if they were responsible for the problem.

We need to start there when discussing the role of the family. Having an eating disorder is nobody's fault, not the child's, the parents', nor the caregivers'. Several factors are necessary, as we've already seen, for this scenario to take place. Assuming a posture of blame and judgment won't help the treatment at all.

Parents need help and care too, because their participation in the treatment process is fundamental. They are the main ones responsible for feeding the children and this sense that they're doing something wrong may even lead them to distance themselves from the situation, as a kind of protective out-of-sight, out-of-mind reflex, which doesn't help anyone.

Surely all parents of children and teens with ARFID have tried everything to get their children eat, right? Despite all the attempts, nothing seems to have worked... So how can parents help their children to eat better?

To talk about the subject, let's consider the following situation. Let's imagine that you, mom or dad, have a terrible fear of heights and that your mother wants to convince you to jump off a diving board that's 30 feet high. So she takes you up to the diving board and tries every type of argument to convince you to jump. She tells you it's going to be fun, that it feels really good, that she'll be proud of you if you jump, that it'll be good for your health, that it'll make you braver, and so on and so forth.

Despite all these arguments, you still don't feel safe jumping. In fact, it seems like the more your mother tries to convince you, the more you don't want to jump. And sometimes you even consider the possibility, to make her happy and calm her down, but you don't have the guts. Because your fear is so great, you keep resisting. Finally, she loses her patience and pushes you off. After getting pushed off the diving board, where you felt terrified, how do you think you'd feel? Scared? Angry? Perhaps betrayed? Even more afraid? And more than that...

- Would you have the courage or the will to show up again at the location of that diving board?
- Will you manage to climb up to the diving board to look down from there ever again?
- Would you ever want to hear any talk about that diving board?
- Would you trust your mother if you ever got up on that diving board again?

Just like in the example of the diving board, when children have ARFID, they can be VERY AFRAID of putting FOOD IN THEIR MOUTH. And when we're afraid, the last thing we want is to feel at risk and experience that same feeling of anguish again.

This is why the more parents pressure their children to eat, the more they refuse to try and, sometimes, end up limiting themselves even further. It's like they're defending themselves or "hiding" in a safe, protected area, and every time someone invades this area uninvited, they expand this space, putting up even stronger barriers so as not to have to again experience the unpleasant feeling they once had. This is probably how things went for you. Your child started by refusing a certain food and this refusal kept expanding to the point of accepting hardly anything.

But if parents can't insist or try to convince their children to eat, what can they do? Most likely, having to stop telling your child to eat brings an overwhelming sense of helplessness, right?!

But just consider: how many times in your life have you argued to convince your child to eat their food? Ten? 100? Maybe 1000 times? And what percentage of the times when you argued did your child actually try a new food? Probably very few or maybe even never, right?

So should parents simply not do anything to try to help?

Maybe you've already gone through phases when you gave up on trying anything new to convince your child to eat and that didn't work either, did it? In fact, when parents give up on everything, they usually leave kids in their totally safe zones, eating foods made specially for them, separated from everyone else, and this most often doesn't work either.

Therefore, parents need to be made aware of their roles and limits so that they can engage and assume the responsibility of offering food that is appropriate for the whole family. Children can't get better on their own.

It's essential for parents to know that even with children who won't agree to eat hardly anything, there are still rules and actions that need to be followed. The role of parents is to ensure that the food structure of the home is respected. This means that even the child who doesn't eat the same foods as the rest of the family has to follow the time rules related to eating and be there at the table at mealtime.

For instance, if a child snacks all day long, they certainly won't have an appetite for trying new foods or eating ones they don't readily accept at mealtime. In addition, if a child eats in their room, or in front of the computer, they're missing the opportunity to become familiar with the foods and learn to accept them.

Promoting family meals is, therefore, a crucial measure in helping children to eat well. We know how challenging this is, since many mothers and fathers work outside of the home all day and are unable to accompany meals, many children study full-time and many families no longer have someone who's responsible for preparing meals, devoting their time to cooking.

We need to face reality, but to also understand that eating is much more than the ingestion of calories and other nutrients and that family meals are essential for promoting a context that encourages a normal, healthy relationship with food. Studies indicate that children and adolescents who more often eat with their family have better quality and variety of food than those that rarely sit down to eat with their parents. These moments are also important for social interaction and the transmission of the family's values. Some studies even suggest that they contribute to protecting against risk behaviors for eating disorders.

Even if parents have little time to eat with their children and are unable to be there for every meal, when they do eat together as a family, they need prioritize and seek meals that are fun and pleasurable, so that their child wants to be with the family and feels good and safe at meals. If these moments are constantly dominated by arguments about eating, then this can be associated with food, making eating acceptance even more difficult.

We know that this might not be easy when a child refuses to eat, generating situations of stress and discomfort for all those involved. We're all human and people may well have outbursts, saying "you don't eat anything," "I don't know what else to do," "you're going to have malnutrition and get sick," "you're too picky with your food" and the like, which can pop out of the mouths of parents and even siblings without them even thinking, sometimes out of exhaustion at going through the same situation and frustration again and again. You shouldn't blame yourself when this happens, but it's important to emphasize that this sort of comment and "labeling" doesn't help, and instead disrupts, leaving the child feeling incapable and guilty.

It's very important to offer words of encouragement or congratulations for an achievement, or else a smile, applause or a hug. Though it's hard to endure the frustration, it's important for parents to "hang in there" and talk about food when offering positive reinforcement and congratulations, but not when blaming and accusing.

Family meals are also essential for providing opportunities to learn how to eat and what to eat. Modeling is one of the main ways of learning through observation—which brings the challenge for parents to be good models, to set an example, to eat the same food that's served to children (even if they still can't eat it). Children imitate adults, so it's important to not make faces or reject food in front of them. This doesn't mean you can't express your preferences, but it's important not to demonize some foods and praise others.

In addition to prioritizing family mealtime, parents can also help their children get to know new flavors and textures by creating opportunities for them to have contact with food. Take your kids to fairs and markets, show them different fruits, vegetables and legumes, encourage them to choose and select certain products, even if they don't eat them, but which are for the family, so they'll have contact with a new food, wash fruits and vegetables to have them ready to be consumed on the table or in the refrigerator, offer lesser accepted foods along with preferred foods, invite the children to cook—all of this helps them to get closer, more familiar and interested in food.

In general, it's important for parents to make sure to stimulate their children, creating a favorable environment, conveying confidence, giving them support and encouraging them to overcome their resistance and fears of facing new situations.

And it's a good idea to be persistent, offering the same food more than once, at different times, and trying out numerous ways to introduce a food (i.e. carrots can be grated, sliced, in sticks, raw, cooked, mixed with rice or meat), because the child may need to be exposed to a certain food's flavor, aroma and texture on several occasions in order for them to get used to it and start accepting it, or so you can actually be sure that the child does not like a particular food.

Many families seek help when they have become discouraged or especially concerned about the situation, and they tend to be exhausted and hopeless, with the feeling that they have tried everything and nothing has worked. And therefore they need to find a treatment space in which they feel welcome, because they will need new energy to embark on the process of treating their child. Don't give up. Follow your intuition (especially mothers) if you notice something and feel like there's something wrong with your child's nutrition, don't wait too long before seeking specialized help. Nutritional deficiencies can take time to take effect, and many pediatricians might say it's "normal" and that it will "pass" as they get a little older, as Fernanda heard so many times.

Treatment should consider the child and their family's biopsychosocial aspects, and be understood as a process that evolves based on the reality of each child and family and which can have advances and setbacks. As Dr. Bacy previously mentioned, this process can be long and time-consuming. But every achievement must be celebrated and worked on in order to be maintained. It's important that the challenges presented to the child can be sustained and supported by the family, but carefully in order not to overburden them and go beyond the limit. The family will always need to learn to deal with the limits and challenges, but with encouragement and support.

SUGGESTIONS TO PARENTS AND CAREGIVERS ABOUT WHAT TO DO AND WHAT NOT TO DO TO HELP CHILDREN WITH ARFID:

DO THIS:

Foster situations in which the child comes in contact with food, for instance, involving them in the process of shopping, preparation, setting the table, going to restaurants, etc.

Ensure the child has a set food structure—in other words, a schedule, setting (sitting at the table) and rules and limits of mealtime (i.e. no TV, tablets, phones, etc.).

Make it a priority to have at least some meals with the whole family every week. Stay calm and collected during meals.

Talk about a variety of subjects and not just food (current events, school, activities, friends, etc).

During meals, put some dishes and ingredients on the table that your child has not yet accepted and some that they already eat and ask that they serve themselves.

Make sure that your child alternates between all the foods that they accept, including the ones they eat but don't love and those they won't always go for.

Talk about the child's acceptance of food as a process.
For example: John doesn't like bananas yet. John is learning to like carrots. John is becoming more secure in trying new foods.

DON'T THIS:

Try to convince the child to try the foods to which they are exposed or those which the family consumes, either through threats, punishments, pressure, arguments about their health, etc.

Allow the child to eat at a time and/or place separate from the family (i.e. in their bedroom, on the couch, in front of the computer). Allow the child to snack between meals.

Argue during meals. Talk only about food and nutrition (i.e. talk about the nutritional content of food or the importance of eating certain foods).

Offer your child a dish prepared only with food that they already accept. Or only put on the table foods that your child is still unable to eat.

Only offer the foods that your child accepts.
Substitute less-accepted foods with more-accepted ones.

Label the child as "the one who doesn't eat anything," "a picky eater" or "fussy."

PART II

VENTING

FERNANDA DO VALLE

Before beginning this second part of the book, in which I will recount the trajectory of my son Theo's food difficulties and the search for help, I would like to state for the record that, from this point on, all the opinions expressed are based on my experience—as a mother—and do not reflect the professional opinions of my co-author Dr. Bacy Fleitlich-Bilyk and our collaborators Manoela Figueiredo and Maria Luiza Petty. I would also like to emphasize that my comments here solely and exclusively refer to treatment approaches for my child. Every individual is unique and what does or does not work for each person has to be evaluated by a professional team along with the family.

Having said that, now let's get going!

As I said in this book's introduction, the decision of whether or not to expose my son's challenges with food was not easy.

But in addition to the reasons already mentioned, the possibility of being able to help other mothers who go through this was one of my strong motivations on this journey.

My own path would have been a lot smoother, or at least lighter, if I there had another mother there to tell me:

"I understand what you're going through." Or a mother embracing me, even if from a distance, welcoming me with empathy, with a simple: "You're not alone."

We mothers—wait, I need to interject something here. If you're a father, please do not feel excluded. In this chapter, I'm referring specifically to mothers because we're the target of most of society's judgment and because there is, in the vast majority of cases, a greater weight on our shoulders.

I have all the respect in the world for fathers who actively participate in their children's lives and are reading this book precisely to try to understand more about this subject and be able to help them.

But back to the point, sometimes we mothers feel unprotected and guilty when there's something going on with our children. Especially when it's something that isn't understood by many people, even people in our family. If even those in the medical field don't know how to deal with ARFID, imagine the "mere mortals" in society.

People judge us and point their fingers, as if it were our fault. After all, it's always Mom's fault, right? What's more, people feel entitled to constantly throw in their two cents, offering you their advice, recipes, prayers and sympathies, as if you hadn't already tried everything.

Of course, there are people with good intentions and good hearts. I shouldn't be unfair.

I got valuable tips from loved ones that made all the difference in my son's development.

Still, the vast majority of people would rather criticize us than actually understand what's going on in order to try to help.

EARLY SIGNS

FERNANDA DO VALLE

My pregnancy with Theo went relatively smoothly. I got sick often in the first 20 weeks, with plenty of nausea and vomiting. I lost weight, but within the normal range for a pregnancy.

He was born at 39 weeks and three days, with a C-section, on September 19, 2011 at 8:07 AM, healthy, weighing 3.51 kilos and measuring 49 centimeters.

He was planned, very much wanted and loved from the start.

Theo came to be the coronation of my healing. He came at a time of celebration, of resurrection, after I had overcome my anorexia.

And the fact that I beat my eating disorder made me think that Theo's own eating would be perfect. After all, now that I had recovered, I would be a great example for him. There was no way to go wrong. It was an absolute certainty. An irrefutable truth.

I was aware of the fact that I had not been a good model for my first son, Daniel, in terms of eating. And although he did not develop any eating disorders, I carried the guilt of him having gone through difficult times by my ARFID—Avoidant/Restrictive Food Intake Disorder side, watching his mother wither away, having difficulty eating, almost losing her life, fighting hard to recover. With Theo, everything would be different. I was going to redeem myself with life.

While still in the maternity ward, everything that I had built in my head started to fall apart.

It seems that Theo was born with a "laziness" for food. He seemed to have little interest in breastfeeding.

Then, at home, we spent two weeks trying, until the doctor, one of those radical types who was very much against the bottle, asked me to start using it. He needed to gain weight and there was no more time to wait.

Along with formula came my feelings of guilt and failure.

Just when we think we have all the answers, Life comes along and changes all the questions.

Absolute truths?

Whoever said there was any such thing?

Those unfunny ironies that come to show us that we have no control over anything and that we still have a lot of learning and growing to do.

And with Theo, I've been learning. He came to teach me.

FOOD INTRODUCTION

FERNANDA DO VALLE

With the introduction of the bottle, Theo accepted the milk well. He began to gain weight and develop well. He was one of those babies covered in little folds of fat—friendly, smiling and happy.

The curious thing is that, if, for whatever reason, we were to change the formula, for another brand, or if some new ingredient was added to the milk that he was used to, he would immediately refuse it. He would make that cute face of disgust that only babies know how to make, refusing to drink.

But as far as the milk he was used to, he would drink it well and with pleasure.

At around four months, we started inserting fruits and juices into his diet. He would spit almost everything out and most of the experiments made him anxious.

He always preferred milk. But we continued offering, insisting (without forcing), knowing that it was at times normal to take a while to get used to the texture of new foods.

Some children take less time, others more, and Theo was certainly in the "more" group.

With soup, it was the same thing. At first, he would spit it out, but after so much insistence, doing handstands, clapping hands, stomping his feet, singing and dancing, he would eat. But he had no interest in eating on his own, in exploring foods. It was always on the basis of distraction. He would open his mouth and "here comes the airplane."

If I left it up to him, he would live off of milk, perhaps even wind or sunlight.

I talked to the pediatrician and his advice was to let Theo go hungry. He instructed me that whenever he didn't want to eat, rather than giving him a bottle, I should just make him wait until the next meal. He assured me that Theo wasn't going to starve. The doctor said that, once the hunger really took hold, he would eat whatever was on his plate and eat it happily.

With much pain in my heart, I did just that, but it didn't work. It was as if he didn't feel the hunger.

I found tips on the internet, from mothers, from nutritionists, from healers, but nothing helped. The only thing I didn't do was call on a witch doctor. I tried everything else.

Another pediatrician went so far to question whether I was a good example for Theo. He suggested that maybe I wasn't the best person to feed him because of my anorexia. I (again) explained to him that I had recovered (I don't think he paid any attention to my words) and he even made sarcastic comments, questioning whether I actually ate food at all.

He ended our consultation by saying that the boy was going to be a picky eater just like his mom.

Well, if anorexia is pickiness, then poor ARFID.

I always took the issue of my eating disorder to his doctors, as a sign of alertness and concern. I felt that something was abnormal about the way he related to food. A mother knows. A mother always knows.

But the doctors didn't seem to take me seriously. None of them tried to understand more or go any deeper.

We always fell into the same cycle of diagnosis: he's just picky, he wants to get attention, he's spoiled, it's a phase, if he goes hungry he'll eat, he'll learn when he goes to school, if he was poor he'd eat...

It got to a point where, having to choose between doing the "right thing" and ensuring he had a minimum of nutrition with milk, I chose to give him milk. I couldn't let the boy starve to death.

I tried to transition him from milk in the bottle to milk in a cup, but he wouldn't accept it. I tried and tested cups of all shapes, colors, materials, some with little animals on them, some with music, with straws, without straws, but nothing worked. So I'd give him the bottle.

I have a strong belief that there's such a thing as the ideal life and then there's real life.

Expectation versus reality. And I confess that I am not one of those so-called "by the book" mothers.

We kept going the way we could manage, not the way we were supposed to. Crucify me if you want! It's fine; it won't be the first time!

But be very careful before you judge a mother who's desperate. Those who are judging today might be mothers tomorrow.

And as the saying goes, don't throw stones.

IMPORTANT

FERNANDA DO VALLE

Before I continue, I'd like to make one point very clear. Just because a person has an eating disorder, this doesn't necessarily mean that their child is going to have one.

This was my case. But I know several mothers (and fathers) who have always had a healthy relationship with food and their bodies, but whose children have ARFID or other eating disorders. I also know mothers who have had eating disorders, but whose children do not.

So if you have or used to have had an eating disorder and are reading this book, don't despair. As Dr. Bacy stated previously, there is no one cause behind the development of ARFID, but rather several factors.

Genetics alone is not fate—after all my elder son has no problem with food. Daniel has always eaten everything.

And though we should never compare one child to another, not even to any other child outside the house, Theo was very different from the average and this caught my attention. It wasn't a question of him not liking one fruit or another, of preferring something to something else. It was a matter of him not liking practically anything, of having zero interest in food and even feeling anxious about the smell or texture of many foods.

I remember at Daniel's first birthday party, we had to keep taking all sorts of things out of his hands—the drumsticks, the cheese balls, the chocolate treats. Without us realizing it, he was attacking the snack trays that passed in front of him. He would squeeze, crumple, smell, put everything in his mouth. He played with the foods. Daniel had a curiosity for food.

But at Theo's first birthday party, at his second birthday party, at his third birthday party, at his fourth birthday party, at his classmates' parties, at all of them, for a long time, he wouldn't eat anything.

He wasn't the one chasing after the snacks and sweets, it was us, his crazed, desperate parents chasing after him, trying to stuff something, anything, into the poor child's mouth.

I just wanted to document that the fact that I had an eating disorder helped me identify that there was something wrong with him. It helped me to insist with the doctors. It was what helped me notice the red flags. But it wasn't the thing, at least not the only thing, that determined that Theo would have ARFID.

ADAPTATION AT SCHOOL

FERNANDA DO VALLE

Just shy of two years of age, Theo started attending school. We opted for the Montessori pedagogical method. There was a great expectation that he would start eating better. The pediatrician insisted that, once he saw other children eating every day, even if in this first phase, only snacks, he would be stimulated to eat better and would also imitate his classmates eating.

It really bothered me when he told me this, because it sounded to me like he was reinforcing the idea that Theo didn't have a good example at home. But I was keeping the faith that this exposure could work.

Adapting was very difficult for Theo. I had to spend a month with him in the classroom. I started leaving very gradually, increasing my time away from the classroom little by little each day.

I even considered taking him out of school, thinking perhaps it was too early for him. He wasn't succeeding in creating a bond with the school.

At the decisive meeting with the team, the psychologist asked me what he most liked to play with. And the answer was:

He likes to play with pressure cooker. Silence hung in the air and I went on:

Not a toy pressure cooker. He likes to play with the real pressure cooker.

Ever since he was little, he had this obsession with pots. But not the kind made for kids. Full-sized pots. He didn't like to eat, but his favorite game was to play cooking.

He spent hours playing with the pots. And he didn't use them to play the drums. He would use them to "cook." He used to pretend he was mixing in spices. He would make the noise of garlic frying with his mouth. He would put in the "ingredients," mix them up and then knock the wooden spoon on the edge of the pot repeatedly, like a master chef.

He didn't have the slightest interest in toys designated for kids his age, so-called "normal" toys.

In attempt to create a bond between Theo and the school, the psychologist decided to buy a pressure cooker and set up an activity with the cooker in the room.

The next day, everything was ready.

It was only after this strategy that he began to develop roots at the school.

It was a sensational plan. It worked.

But the strategy of exposing him to other children eating for his own eating to improve was a failure.

Not only did he have zero interest in what his classmates were eating, he also gave the other kids whatever he had in his lunchbox.

He was a goodhearted boy who had learned, from an early age, to break bread with his "brothers and sisters."

Beautiful in the Christian context—but, in my desperation, tragic in the context of food.

And even though he would play all morning at school and not eat his snack, when he got home he wouldn't want to have lunch. It was always the same struggle. If it were up to him, he would only go for his beloved bottle.

"Operation Eat Better at School" had failed to take off. Mission failed.

THE ACCIDENT

FERNANDA DO VALLE

As a mother, my greatest fear in terms of my children has always been that they would get hurt. I believe that every mother has her own personal nightmare. Some are afraid that their child will fall ill, others that they will stop breathing in their sleep, that they'll choke on something, and so on. My fear—or rather, my panic—was that they would injure themselves or be injured by someone, especially at school or when I wasn't around. I had this false sensation that I could always protect them.

When they weren't with me, obsessive thoughts would invade my mind, consuming me with images of horrible accidents. I would hear an ambulance and immediately imagine it was one of my kids lying on the stretcher inside.

And in the period when Theo was adapting to school (as was I), this emotional limitation of mine was on edge.

In this context, life taught me yet another great lesson.

On a Sunday night, while I was in the kitchen making dinner for Daniel, Theo, with his never-ending energy, was excitedly running around the house.

When I finished putting Dani's plate in the oven, Theo ran right past me, doing his best impression of an F1 race car.

My heart skipped, perhaps sensing what was about to come, and I implored him:

Slow down son.

Like a good son, who never listens to his mother, he sped up a little.

He dashed into the hallway like it was the home stretch of some big race.

His dad was right behind him.

From where I was standing, I could see the two of them. I was watching as he, with nothing in his way to trip over, fell to the ground. He fell on his face, with a pacifier, hitting his mouth.

His father immediately picked him up. Theo was screaming in pain. His crying was high-pitched, pained in a way he'd never cried before.

I ran over to see what had happened and, when I got near, all I could see was blood, and lots of it, pouring out of his little mouth.

My husband went to the kitchen, turned on the faucet and started washing his mouth. But the blood wouldn't stop flowing. We took him straight to the emergency room.

His upper front tooth had been jammed into his gums. His smile had gotten a little window with the lights out. And in addition, it had cut his labial frenulum. That's what was causing the uninterrupted bleeding. As for the frenulum, there was nothing that could be done. It would heal back over time. They stopped the bleeding, without any stitches. And the tooth was going to have to be evaluated by a specialist the next day, and that's what we did. We took him to my cousin Marina, who was the boys' dentist at the time. She reassured us saying that the tooth had merely entered the gum. It hadn't broken in there and apparently had not been permanently compromised.

She said that, in time, the little tooth would reposition itself and come back down until it reached its normal position. And that is in fact what happened. The tooth came down and lined up nicely.

I had never associated this accident with Theo's mouth with ARFID. It was only when I read about ARFID that I learned that the eating disorder could be associated with a trauma that a person experienced—choking, for instance—that I took a few steps back and made this connection.

In Theo's case, the trauma wasn't specific to food, but it was related to the mouth, the canal through which we are fed.

Of course, as I said earlier, Theo already had difficulty eating. But after studying more on the subject, I noted that, after this episode, it got worse. Maybe this is what accelerated things. Was it the missing trigger? I don't know for sure, but this brings us back to the idea that a number of combined factors contribute to the development of an eating disorder. It's not an isolated thing.

For a few days, his mouth was completely swollen, and the solid food (the little that he did eat) was suspended. The beloved bottle was the only thing he accepted.

At the time of this accident, I got really down. I wanted to put him inside of a bubble, so he'd never get hurt ever again. So that he couldn't run anymore.

I would wake up in the middle of the night sweating, having terrible thoughts, seeing images of Theo's bloody mouth. I had countless panic attacks.

I kept reliving the scene, punishing and tormenting myself with the thought: "I could have prevented it." "His dad could have prevented it."

It's amazing how we mothers are able to torture themselves with guilt. I was so afraid of him getting hurt at school, when it happened right in front of us, at home, with nothing dangerous in his path. It was his fall that made the least sense and the one that hurt him the most.

Ironies of life... Ironies that happen for a reason. Things of destiny that take place to make us reflect.

I think that whenever something happens to us, we need to look at the situation closely, and very honestly ask ourselves: "What is it that life wants to teach me with this?"

Reflecting, I realized that there is a very fine line between protection and control.

It's a subtle boundary, but we need to understand the difference. Being a mother is a difficult mission, an arduous task that is assigned to us and doesn't come with an instruction manual. It's a constant learning experience, a whirlwind of strong emotions.

And if there is one thing in life of which I am certain it is that I will continue to stumble in this challenging and complex role of being a mother.

Stumbling is inevitable. It's part of our growth. But mothers always get up and push ahead. After all, as I said before, mothers don't give up.

THE CHANGE

FERNANDA DO VALLE

When Theo was three, my husband got an offer from the company he worked for to take a position in the United States. We don't think twice—at least, I don't think we did. We packed up and moved there with the boys.

Since I had always wanted to live in the land of Uncle Sam and the boys were studying at the American School of Campinas, our adaptation was in general a very smooth one.

The hardest part was Theo's eating. In Brazil, I had help in the kitchen and at home.

Even though he would eat very little, the little he did eat was food that Ivete made, and that he used to.

Ivete was the angel who had worked in my house since I was nine. When I got married, she came with me. I "stole" her from my mother's house. She always helped me a lot with my kids. It was a relationship of coexistence that lasted for nearly 30 years. She was family.

Incidentally, at the time when the pediatrician suggested that, because I had an eating disorder, maybe I wasn't the best person to feed my son and deal with his eating difficulties, I delegated a good part of his food to her.

I believed the pediatrician, thinking I was a failure as a mother. I thought I was incapable of doing even the most basic task. I was unable of feeding my own child.

When we announced that we were moving, the question inevitably came up: "How are you going to get this boy to eat there without help?"

Of course, this made me feel bad and I wondered if I could actually do it.

But I stopped listening to people and started listening to my heart and my power to overcome.

And moving here was the best thing that ever happened to me. When we have a lot of help at home, we end up accommodating ourselves to some tasks and we become accommodated to our limitations. We have a plan B, a plan C... We don't go outside of our comfort zone. We don't need to.

But in the United States, I only had Plan F. And Fernanda was forced to get by on her own.

I had no other option. With no help at home, I had to face my ghosts and fears.

I went into the kitchen. I learned how to cook. I learned to cook the things that he used to eat in Brazil. I also sought out new recipes and new alternatives. Inside the house, we were adapting, and within his selectivity, Theo would eat the little he could take every day.

The problem started to get worse when the time came for him to go to school.

We also chose a Montessori school for him in the US. As he had studied at this type of school in Brazil, I opted for the same philosophy, so he'd have an easier time adapting.

Theo started pre-K on the eve of his fourth birthday. We arrived in the United States in early 2015 and he had private lessons at home until the beginning of the school year in September.

When I went to see the principal, at the time of enrollment, I talked about my concerns about my little boy's eating.

At this school, all the kids ate the same snack. Each week, one family would bring in a snack for the whole class, selected from a list that the school provided. Each family was responsible for the snacks twice a year.

Although the snack was collective, each student had the autonomy to decide when they would eat (this is part of the Montessori concept, creating independence and responsibility).

Food was available during a period of the morning, and each child would eat when they were hungry or felt like eating.

Needless to say, he always chose not to eat at all. He was never hungry nor did he feel like eating.

I talked with his teacher and we agreed that every day there would be a cup of goldfish crackers available for Theo. These are toasted cheddar cheese-flavored snacks that Theo agreed to eat and they were on the school's list of permitted foods.

I was very reluctant to ask for this, as I didn't want him to be given special treatment and be seen as being "different" by his classmates. I was afraid of him getting bullied.

But it was much more important that he eat. This had to be placed above any prejudice, including my own.

And more important than having the snacks available was that the teacher remind Theo to eat. Although this went against the school's philosophy, everyone was very kind to me and accommodated him in this difficulty, without judgment.

But there was one other catch. In Brazil, he used to only go to school in the morning, but here in the US, he had to go at least three times a week until 2:45 PM. In other words, he'd have to have lunch there too.

I asked the principal to let him come home for lunch. There was no way he could go so much time without eating anything. I was worried. I knew he was going to spend a lot more energy than he would ingest.

She insisted that he stay in school the regular time. She asked that we at least try. And I was ready to give up before we even got started—that instinct to protect which sometimes makes us want to put our children in the famous bubble of "safety."

The principal said he might be stimulated by the other children. I already knew that this was unlikely to happen, but she was right, I couldn't give up before trying.

She also told me that he would come home hungry and it would help him eat better. Based on prior experience, I didn't put much faith in this strategy, but I thought a lot about everything she said and decided it might be good. After all, this was another time. "Who knows, now that he's gotten older, it might work," I thought hopefully.

Each child brought their own food for lunch. I tried sending in everything, or rather everything of the few foods he liked. But the containers almost always came back the same way they were sent in: full.

Theo always had something very particular, which many label as pickiness, but later on, understanding his difficulty eating and that there might be a sensory sensitivity associated with this difficulty, it all made sense. Notice these peculiarities, because everything will fall into place further on.

For example, he would eat bean soup with noodles at home. But when I would send the very same soup, prepared the same way, in his thermos, he would say that it wasn't the same. And indeed it wasn't. It actually was, but, inside the thermos, the soup tasted different than the soup he ate in a bowl at home. That was enough for him not to eat it. The smell changed. The texture changed. The temperature changed. And he wouldn't eat it. He couldn't get it down.

The same was true of milk. He would drink milk from his bottle. In a cup, the flavor would change, making him anxious. I reported in another chapter that, while we were still in Brazil, I had tried to transfer the milk to a cup and tried with all possible types of material. I tried again here in the US—and the cups they have here do everything except actually make the child drink—but nothing worked.

Whenever I sent him a sandwich for lunch, plain sliced bread with a little butter, wrapped in aluminum foil, plastic wrap, a napkin or in a little container, it changed the flavor for him, and he had difficulty eating it. He'd take a few nibbles and stop.

Things he liked that came prepackaged and that he would eat or drink straight from the packaging were easier for him, as these variations in taste and texture did not occur. But he hardly liked anything that came like that. We'd go back to the goldfish, which was already his morning snack.

I got so desperate that I would pick him up with a bottle of milk in the car. I was afraid he would faint from weakness.

I no longer cared, as I mentioned before. It had been a long time since I cared about what was right or wrong. When we're talking about our children's actual lives, there are things that work and things that don't. There's no such thing as right and wrong.

My concern was ensuring that he was getting the minimum amount of calories and nutrients for him to develop.

But time was going by and he was becoming more selective and restrictive with each passing day.

My last shot, in the hope that life would help solve it, that life would lend us a hand, and that this difficulty would disappear like magic, didn't work.

I confess I was hoping for a miracle at his new school in the US. I put in all my chips on that change.

Sometimes mothers would rather hope for a miracle than have to face up and admit to a problem. It's easier to wait for life to work things out than to get involved.

But the time had come to accept that this wasn't going to pass on its own, that it wasn't a phase, that the school wasn't going to solve the problem and that seeing other kids eat wasn't going to do the magic that I had hoped for.

The fact that Theo was with other children eating, in another country, at another time, in another school, at other times, in another context, didn't help and nothing changed.

And him coming home, after a day having eaten practically nothing at all, also didn't make him eat whatever was on his plate.

It was in this context that I started the most important part of this process. I couldn't push any longer. It was time to face and accept the truth. But awareness alone doesn't generate change.

It was necessary to act and seek help.

Or rather, to fight for help. And for him.

I asked for the school if they could recommend a good pediatrician and thus we began the long process that helped us to arrive at the diagnosis that changed our lives.

To be continued...

PEDIATRICS IN THE US

FERNANDA DO VALLE

As I said before, because of the fact that I had an eating disorder, I suspected that Theo had one. Because of everything I went through, everything I studied, for all the experience I accumulated in helping others, I knew he had something more than just selectivity.

I even thought about anorexia, but there were a lot of things that didn't fit the clinical scenario. He wasn't concerned with his body shape. He wasn't afraid of getting fat. He didn't demonstrate a desire to lose weight. He didn't have body image distortion or obsessive thoughts. So I considered Eating Disorders Not Otherwise Specified (EDNOS), which, as the description states, is the diagnosis given to cases that do not meet all the criteria. Until he turned seven, I had never read about or heard of ARFID.

My greatest fear, incidentally, due to genetic predisposition, was that he would develop anorexia as he got older. Many people may not be aware of this, but anorexia has become more common in men. Today, more studies are being done and there is more research data on this. It's not just a woman's disease, as many believe.

And since I was also an extremely selective child and this selectivity may have contributed to triggering the process of my anorexia, I was terrified that my history would repeat itself in him.

When I went to the pediatrician here in the US with all these details about my history, my concerns with Theo's eating, he was extremely nurturing, reacting in a manner completely different from all the pediatricians that I had consulted in Brazil.

In the first consultation we had here to discuss this subject, Theo was four years old. It was right after he started school, in the middle of the process described in the previous chapter.

The pediatrician didn't mention ARFID. He diagnosed Theo as a picky eater. But here people don't view this as a simple lack of openness. They take it quite seriously. I wasn't subjected to judgment, nor was Theo.

We were received with warmth for the first time in four years. And even without the correct diagnosis, this in itself was a relief. It took a load off my back. Just having someone listening to me, without making faces, felt soothing. I felt as if I were being cradled in my mother's arms.

The pediatrician listened to Theo attentively. He listened to the short list of foods he ate and got him to agree to some arrangements.

I talked about my concerns with him staying at school while hardly eating anything and he was brilliant.

He recommended that I try to give him a heavier breakfast, but without forcing anything and keeping in mind that his stomach was much smaller than mine, and asked me not to worry so much about what he ate at school. He suggested that he have lunch after he got home, even though that would be at three in the afternoon, and that he should continue to eat more from that time until he went to sleep. He told me to "reverse" his day. He would have small snacks at school and meals at home. He asked me not to worry about the diversity of his food at that time, but instead with the minimal amount of calories needed for him to continue growing and developing. He recommended a supplement to help supply vitamins that he was not getting from his food and asked that I schedule an appointment with a nutritionist specializing in picky eaters to help work on his selectivity.

Another issue that I brought up at that same consultation and which, at that time, I did not know was linked to his food selectivity, is that the school had detected a delay in Theo's fine motor skills.

He showed difficulty in holding his pencil correctly when writing and coloring. He didn't have the hand strength to cut with scissors or mold Play-Doh with the same agility as other children his age. To summarize, he didn't have the same ability to perform certain activities with his hands.

The pediatrician also did not make any association at that time. He only recommended that I start occupational therapy as soon as possible so that his hands could be strengthened and he would catch up to his classmates (I'll come back to this later with more info on how all this may be connected).

I left the office with a recommendation for a nutritionist, an occupational therapist and much more. I left with hope.

There's no better feeling in this world than a getting warm reception without judgment.

BEGINNING TREATMENT

FERNANDA DO VALLE

As soon as we left the consultation with the pediatrician, I made appointments with the recommended professionals to begin treatment as soon as possible.

The following week, the occupational therapist started accompanying him at school in 30-minute sessions twice a week.

She developed an itinerary to meet his needs, but in a light, playful manner. She was able to win him over in the first days and he committed himself, cooperating with the treatment.

The therapist accompanied him for two years, and even during school vacation, she continued to attend him at our home in order to maintain his therapy. Summer vacation lasts three months here in the US, so that would have been a long time for him to go unaccompanied.

It was excellent work and extremely necessary. Along with the occupational therapy, he also started playing the piano to help strengthen his fingers.

At the time, I had no idea that this delay in Theo's fine motor coordination was linked to the fact that he had skipped a few steps in the process of learning to eat and that all of this was also connected, as I'll explain a little later on, to a flaw in his sensory processing.

As Theo had no interest in food, he never explored it. If it were up to him, he would never eat. I could put a colorful, well-designed dish in front of him, with all the shapes seen in the nutrition and recipe books for children, but nothing would pique his interest. So Theo never had that basic phase of starting to eat on his own. If it didn't fall into his mouth, he simply wouldn't eat it. He neither practiced nor developed his fine motor coordination. This, combined with the fact that kids today are less stimulated by manual activities than by using tablets and electronic devices, made it necessary for us to try to repair the harm done.

When he started first grade, at age six, he no longer needed this accompaniment and was actually advanced in writing compared to other children in the same age group.

Because of all of his eating difficulties, Theo also didn't properly develop his ability to chew. For many years, he had difficulty chewing harder things, even demonstrating a fear of breaking his teeth. And I, Fernanda, his mother, far from being a professional, believe that this fear of his is also linked to the accident he had with his mouth, described in a previous chapter.

But I only arrived at all these associations after I learned about ARFID, a little later on in our lives.

As such, this matter needs to be further explored. If I had known all this before, I would have sought help sooner and could have minimized the harm to Theo's development.

I actually did seek help earlier, but, unfortunately, the healthcare professionals didn't know how to address it.

So let me reformulate the last paragraph: if the healthcare professionals had known all this, we could have, together, minimized the harm to Theo's development.

Now we can move ahead!

I had the first consultation with the nutritionist by myself. I told him my entire history. I talked about his relationship with food and brought the short list of what he ate and drank, which at the time was:

- milk (only in a baby's bottle and Ninho 1+[1], which, where I live, can only be found at one place, causing me to stock up on cans like I was preparing for some apocalyptic storm);
- lemonade (only one specific brand and, of course, a brand that's especially hard to find);
- omelets (only when made by my husband. Whenever I made one, even telling him that his dad made it, he would know and refuse to eat);
- bean soup with pasta (only a specific brand of beans and one format of pasta, also a specific brand, and he would only eat the soup when I made it. If his dad made it and told him it was me, he would know and refused to eat);
- cornmeal cake (made by his father);
- oatmeal cookie (only the kind his father makes, and it had to be on the soft side);
- goldfish crackers (only one flavor).

This was what he ate in his daily routine. And he had eaten these same exact things for years. Rain or shine, summer or winter, it was always the same. Normally it was the bean soup for lunch (when he wasn't at school) and the omelet for dinner. But, if his father was traveling, which he often did, since Theo wouldn't eat my omelet, it would be soup for lunch and dinner. His father once spent two weeks away from home and he had bean soup for lunch and dinner two weeks straight. Whenever I had to travel, I would make a batch of soup before I left. But there was something about the way his father heated it up that made it different and he would refuse to eat. Over time, he gradually learned to tolerate these "differences" and was able to

---
1. Ninho 1+ is a brand of milk formula sold by Nestlé, which claims to have developed the product especially for one-year-old toddlers and up.

eat my soup even when his father heated it up. But he would never eat an omelet when I made it, even when I followed his dad's recipe to a T.

Dr. Marsha Dunn Klein, occupational therapist, a reference in childhood eating disorders in the US would say that Theo has a parentheses diet, meaning that the specific foods listed in said diet come with "requirements"—of the shapes, the brands, the person who prepares it, the color, etc.—in parentheses.

Once he made it out of the baby soup phase (he would only accept two flavors), that's what we were able to introduce and that's what he stayed with for many years. He didn't get any closer, nor did he try anything other than what's on this list. Eventually, he started eating bread with olive oil when we would go to a specific restaurant, or a little plain rice, or a little plain pasta, no sauce or anything else, and with much effort. And he liked popcorn, but only on occasion. And it wasn't just any popcorn. It had to be a specific brand, cooked at an exact time in the microwave, etc. And every now and then he would eat vanilla ice cream, also one specific brand.

The nutritionist advised me based on the diagnosis of childhood food selectivity. And although she also hadn't considered ARFID, she provided me with an approach that started to help us in this process.

It was a treatment based on the division of responsibilities, an approach developed by nutritionist Ellyn Satter. I would choose what and where he would eat (preferably at the table with the whole family, at the same time as everyone else), and he would choose how much he would eat and whether he was going to eat.

Of course, I needed to make an adjustment to this concept. I made him agree that he would eat at least a minimal amount. Because if we kept the "whether he was going to eat" criterion, he simply wouldn't eat.

She suggested that I always offer three food options, and that one of the options had to be something he was already used to eating, something from his short list of safe foods.

For example, omelets were something he would already eat. So I would give him an omelet, a carrot and three or four peas. Of the things he still wouldn't eat, the suggestion was to give him only a very little. In this case, the deal was that he would have to eat at least some of his omelet. He wouldn't have to try or even touch whatever it is that he didn't eat, if he didn't want to.

Initially, the idea of this technique was for him to learn to tolerate eating while there were new foods near him, preferably on his plate. He had an aversion to the smell of a lot of things and would feel anxious just being near them. And this made it very difficult to use this approach.

It wasn't easy to get Theo to agree to start trying. Let's remember that at that time he was four, an age when children, even those who have no problem with eating may exhibit a sudden selectivity and refusal to try and accept new foods. This fear of eating something new, known as food neophobia, explained by Manoela and Maria Luiza at the beginning of the book, when not associated with any other discomfort or other causes also presented by the nutritionist contributors to this work, usually passes spontaneously and without causing harm to the child. This unfortunately was not Theo's case, as we will see in the coming chapters.

After many conversations, he agreed to begin trying, but on the condition that we use the sort of plates that have divided sections. One food couldn't come in contact with another. If a pea happened to touch his omelet, goodbye omelet. It would "contaminate" his food.

What he really liked was having just the omelet on his plate. I noticed that he was more tense and agitated when there was something else on his plate, even though he knew he didn't have to eat it.

I would alternate. One day, I'd put it on his plate. The next, I'd leave it on the table, near him, but not on his plate. And we went on like this for some time. But since he ended up eating better when the other new foods weren't near him, and this exposure wasn't instilling any spontaneous interest in him, I ended up deciding to abort this plan and allowing him to eat the things he was used to.

The only new thing he tried during this period was an apple, peeled and cut into small pieces. He showed zero curiosity for everything else.

The tactic had helped a little in terms of his toleration of certain smells, but it had not been successful in stimulating his curiosity, much less bringing results in him trying new things.

There was more to it than selectivity. There was fear, anxiety and aversion. Eating wasn't something that brought him pleasure. It was like a chore. Hunger was rare. And he used an unusual vocabulary to describe certain things. He would say that a banana was dirty, that it was rotten and he had never eaten a rotten banana, or a dirty one.

I remember when he was two years old, trying to eat a minuscule piece of lettuce, he said that it was disgusting. And, at least at home, he had never heard anyone say that. Fine, you might say that lettuce isn't the best option for most kids, but he would say the same thing about chocolate.

And at the time that he was four years old, he went through a phase in which he would cry in desperation, not wanting to drink or eat anything, saying that he was afraid that the drink and the food would go to his heart and make him sick. To this day, I don't know where he got this idea and where this panic came from. It was a very difficult time, in which I had to turn to a psychologist in order to help calm him down when he had these crises. He gradually got better and forgot about this subject.

There are lots of things that Theo didn't like eating, but of the few things he did like, he would eat just a little and then say he was full. He often complained that his belly hurt.

And if he did eat a little more, it seemed that his body couldn't take it, and he would either vomit or have diarrhea.

Of course, all of this generated discomfort in him, both physical and emotional. These were not positive experiences with food.

We did a number of tests and they showed no functional or structural problems in his gastrointestinal system.

And even with all the clinical examinations indicating that there was nothing wrong with Theo, my heart was restless and my maternal instinct told me that there was something that had not yet been identified.

AT LONG LAST, THE DIAGNOSIS

FERNANDA DO VALLE

From age four to six, Theo was treated as having food selectivity, though, as I mentioned in the previous chapter, this did not make complete sense to me. I wasn't comfortable with this. My heart was not at peace and I didn't see any significant improvements in his eating. There was a piece missing from the puzzle.

I continued going to the nutritionist. She worked only with me, giving me the guidelines. Theo didn't participate in the consultations. This was her approach. She didn't want to stress him out unnecessarily. I wondered what it would take for it to be necessary. Nevertheless…

He continued seeing the same pediatrician and, as he got older, without any compromise to his physical development, doing well in school and not having any problems with socialization, there were no concerns.

Theo's weight, starting from age four, when he first started to sprout up, was always at the minimum limit. With rare exceptions, he was never below the minimum. This only happened when he had a virus or the flu, because since he was always at this limit and because he ate very selectively, he lost weight easily. He lost weight easily and took a long time to gain weight. This was to be expected.

But, thank God, Theo hardly ever got sick—which was a big help because he had nothing in the way of reserves, not nutrients nor extra "meat on his bones."

In Theo's case, though he had no problem socializing, eating in social situations always generated discomfort, since there was hardly ever any of the foods he liked to eat at his friends' birthday parties. And the kids' parties here aren't like the buffets they have in Brazil. Here, the parties are only two hours long and a half-hour before they end, the children gather at the table and share some pizza or something which the family serves. Then comes the cake or cupcakes and then the party's over. In other words, there's no way for him to fake it. At the table, it was evident that he didn't eat. As he got older, the other children began to notice and make comments. He had a number of embarrassing experiences.

The craziest thing about this whole thing is that, whenever other mothers realized that he hadn't eaten, either at the birthday parties or at a friend's house, they would question me:

Does he eat pizza?
No.
Does he eat hot dogs or burgers?
No.
Wait! Does that mean he doesn't eat chocolate, cupcakes, sweets, candy? Doesn't drink soda? Doesn't eat ice cream?
No.
Oh, how wonderful! That must be why he's so skinny. If only my child were like that!

What? Take it from me, lady: you definitely do not want your child to be like that. It's not a question of him not eating what people consider to be junk food. Food isn't just about whether it's healthy or not. Food is also part of social life. It is part of our affective memories. And there's no problem with eating all these things that people consider "forbidden" every once in a while. It's a part of life.

My God! This is one thing that's insane about our society. It seems like everything revolves around being skinny. Only the fat kids are viewed as problematic, as being sick. Weight and physical appearance do not define health. How long are we going to tolerate this kind of judgment?

Also furthermore, lady, you also don't know how embarrassing it is for your child to be in the home of a friend, or their parents' friends, or a family member, and to be offered a thousand things to eat only for the child to say no to every option. There's a tension in the air. The host doesn't know what to do and what else to offer to try to please.

I've already been through a thousand and one situations in which our hosts felt more awkward than I did (as both a selective child and adult, as well as the mother of a selective child).

Obviously, I never made this speech whenever someone would blurt out, "Oh! How wonderful that he doesn't eat any of this stuff." Today, now that I know about his ARFID, I try to explain carefully and politely in order to help people to understand, stop judging and labeling children and adults alike. And if they can't understand it, to at least learn to respect it.

But does it make me want to curse them out like I just came down with a case of Tourette's? Sure, it does! Another limitation that comes from Theo's selectivity affects our ability to travel. We've always had to pack a "basic survival kit" of his safe foods.

This is why I'm insisting here that you shouldn't just consider the possibility of ARFID, or any other eating disorder for that matter, when a person is underweight. It's also necessary to think about the other disadvantages and limitations that their eating causes, not only for the individual, but also their family as a whole.

If you're a mother and feel like something doesn't add up in terms of what the doctors are saying, follow your intuition and don't give up looking for help.

Eventually, it will come. Just like it did for us!

Until he was almost seven years old, Theo's diet was largely based on milk (in the bottle). He would also eat the bean soup, omelettes and the other items I listed, but always in small amounts, and I inevitably had to complement it with milk, out of fear that he wouldn't get the minimum daily calories he needed to develop.

I had two major concerns about Theo's food selectivity. Once he started playing sports more, the numbers wouldn't add up (caloric intake versus caloric expenditure). Here in the United States, school sports are taken very seriously and the practice sessions are intensive. I knew that, based on what he consumed, his weight could drop. And my other concern was in getting rid of the bottle. Since I had tried unsuccessfully on several occasions to transfer his milk from the bottle to a cup, I needed to count on the possibility of him rejecting the milk. I needed to have a plan B ready.

I had put it off long enough. The time had come and we couldn't wait any longer. Since we were about to move into a new home, and along with this change, he'd be starting at a new school, a big school for "big boys," we made a deal that the bottles would stay at our "old house." We made this arrangement with a good amount of time for him to assimilate. And during that time, I was trying to get him to try some dairy products, something other than milk that could push up his protein and calorie intake.

When we moved, it was just as I predicted. Said and done. After I got rid of the bottle, he never put another drop of milk in his mouth. He only tried it again a long time later, but after having refused it a lot, in the process of exposure techniques, which was part of the treatment he was undergoing. I'll tell you more about this approach a little later on.

We managed to substitute the milk with Danoninho[1] yogurt drink. Only one flavor, and of course the one that's most difficult to find.

And him no longer drinking milk out of the bottle didn't mean he was going to eat any more food. Not even the pediatricians' thesis applied this time. I managed to make some minimal increases. He started drinking more lemonade. And since he took well to olive oil, I was able to up his caloric intake by putting more in his soup. Squeezing in a few calories here and there, with a lot of effort and sweat, I gave him the minimum he needed.

After all these changes, new home, new school, no more milk from the bottle, just when I didn't know what else to do, one day, talking to two close friends of mine who had been diagnosed with anorexia (but both of whom had always had the feeling that the diagnosis didn't make sense in their lives), I heard about ARFID for the first time. They had just read about the subject and, for the first time in their lives, they felt there was a REAL explanation for all of their suffering with food. They were familiar with and had accompanied Theo's story and, because they identified with many things, they sent me the articles of the most important discovery of their lives, which soon became the most important of my life too. For them and for him.

I devoured all the material and did more research, diving in headfirst. And before discussing it with the pediatrician, I already knew. It all made sense. Every word. Every sentence. Every description. That was IT. It had a name with just a few letters. A few letters that brought great clarification.

With this new information in hand, I made an appointment with the pediatrician, to get a new evaluation. Because of one of those coincidences of life, of God, of the Universe or whatever you

---

1. Danoninho is a French brand of cheese-based fermented pulp with added fruits and minerals popular with Brazilian children in the 80s and 90s.

want to call it, the pediatrician who had always attended Theo was not available. I made an appointment with another pediatrician at the clinic. An angel named Dr. Pugh.

He was extremely caring doctor with Theo. He listened to me attentively and confirmed the diagnosis: Theo officially had ARFID. This new pediatrician has a child with eating difficulties and he understood Theo's struggle, as a doctor and as a father. He empathized with our suffering and received us without judgment. The first thing the doctor told me, after confirming the diagnosis:

It's not your fault and it's not his fault.

The second thing he said was, *"Children with ARFID don't imitate other children eating, so their own eating doesn't improve when they go to school. And it's no use sending food he doesn't like in his lunchbox, thinking that one day he's going to open it up and miraculously try it."*

And he explained to me that it wasn't just a behavioral issue. There was a physical issue involved, an associated sensory sensitivity that brought about all of his difficulties with food. The pediatrician talked about the three subtypes of ARFID, which Dr. Bacy previously explained, and Theo fit all three. He had the complete package.

When the doctor talked about the symptoms of sensory sensitivity in the context of ARFID, he explained that this sensitivity often affects all senses, not just the palate. And based on that information, I was really able to make the connection between many things that now, literally, made sense. Not everyone with ARFID exhibits sensory issues, but it's quite common.

As I previously described, Theo has always had a very sensitive sense of smell, often getting anxious just from the scent of something, not being able to be near anyone who was eating, and this made it difficult for us, as a family, to model for him at the table, because he couldn't even be close to us. It also made it difficult to expose him to many foods, because he couldn't tolerate their scent.

Theo's hearing has always been more sensitive too. I remember the first time I took Theo to a children's carnival in Brazil.

The other children were jumping, dancing, screaming, and there he was, standing with both hands over his ears, horrified by all the noise. I have so many pictures of him at birthday parties, while everyone's singing "Happy Birthday," just like that, hands clamped over his ears. He always complained that his classmates spoke too loudly in the classroom and in the cafeteria at lunch—things most children don't mind. Even when I'd ask him why he didn't finish his lunch at school, he would say because it was too loud. And I would tell him that one thing had nothing to do with the other (at that time I didn't know about this relationship).

His vision has always been more sensitive too. He was bothered by brightness more than the average child. He would say that his eyes hurt, that they were burning, and he wasn't able to stay outdoors in the sun in some situations. Right away, he would look for some shady spot, stay there for a while as if callibrating his vision, and then go back to playing. I remember the first time I took him to Disney World. He was almost three and he spent most of our time in the parks sitting in his stroller, the kind that had an umbrella. He pulled down that little sun-breaker visor, so it covered his whole face. He wasn't at all interested in Mickey. And it was his mom who came off as Goofy.

And it was no different with his sense of touch. If he touched any little thing, he would say his hands were "sticky" and run to go wash them. And it wasn't enough to wipe them on a napkin or a tissue. He needed to wash them with water and a lot of soap. He would open the trash bin with his feet (the kind with the hand mechanism, in the homes here in the US), something he didn't learn at home. He looked like a ninja opening the trash. And no, he doesn't have OCD. I used to worry about that, too.

These symptoms are linked to sensory sensitivity, which is part of ARFID. Either that or ARFID is part of this sensitivity. Each treatment approach has its own position on this. I don't know exactly which triggered which, or in what order it happened, and it doesn't matter. The important thing is to learn how to deal with it to minimize the child's discomfort. In another chapter, I'll explore this in greater detail. Further on, we discovered still other things associated with this whole scenario. I'll be back with more information that came in the course of these findings. When I opened up about Theo's ARFID on my social media and talked about his sensory sensitivity, a lot of people asked me if he was autistic, because this hypersensitivity is often found in autism. And even after explaining that he wasn't on the spectrum and that his symptoms were mild compared to the sensory difficulties present in autism, I still received hundreds of messages suggesting, or rather, stating that he was indeed autistic (from laypeople who see themselves as experts and from experts who feel entitled to give their opinion without knowing the whole story). Many of these messages accused me, saying that I was in denial of his autism.

I know that when we expose ourselves we're subjected to criticism and the opinions of others. Both good and bad come with the package. But I'm amazed at the way people judge, put their finger in your face, give diagnoses and even label their fellow human based on nothing more than the logic of "because I think so."

If my son were autistic, I would have no problem with that. I would be the first to accept him with love and affection, the exact same way that I accept his ARFID and I will always accept him in any difficulty he may face in life.

These "absolute truths" created by people, including doctors, this prejudice that surrounds us, make it so difficult to seek treatment and help.

More love, please people!

If you don't want to understand, at least, learn to respect.

Now back to the consultation, once I received Theo's diagnosis, after all the explanations from the pediatrician, a sense of relief came over me. How soothing it was to hear things that made sense.

The only reason I didn't the doctor is because, here in the United States, there is more of a physical distancing that is cultural and it would have caused the doctor a great deal of embarrassment. But I used words to express what I felt in my heart at that moment.

He explained to me what the treatment would be like in practice from that moment on, gave me the guidelines and I left feeling like I was on cloud nine.

The diagnosis alone does not change the scenario, nor does it cure anyone. But it does give us a light, a hope, an understanding and a way forward.

Comfort. Happiness.

Of course, I wasn't happy because my son had an eating difficulty.

But because I got this validation. An explanation.

Just gratitude!

THE PATH

FERNANDA DO VALLE

Theo was diagnosed with ARFID shortly after he turned seven. And after this reassessment of his eating difficulty, the treatment changed. We continued for another year following the Exposure Therapy line, as part of the Cognitive-Behavioral Therapy approach.

We would choose, always together with him, some foods for him to challenge himself, foods with which he had difficulty, but which he wanted to learn to tolerate and like, either because it was good for his health, or because it was something easy to take to school, or because it was something offered to him at his friends' houses and at parties, and easily accessible things that we could find while traveling. Our choices always considered the social aspect.

In the beginning, he would try two new foods per week. It's a very slow process that requires lots of love and patience.

First, he learned to tolerate being near the new food. Then he would touch it and explore it (he had skipped that phase as a baby, remember?). When he would visually observe and explore the food through touch, he had to describe it, without judgments. He couldn't, for example, say it was disgusting, good or bad. Instead he would describe the color, the texture, the shape, say whether looking at that food made him remember anything.

These are techniques that help children to change focus and relax before trying a new food. We also used breathing techniques to lower his anxiety.

Then he would smell it and only in the last stage would he put the food in his mouth and sometimes, in this first attempt, he would just lick it. He wasn't obligated to swallow. If he needed to spit it out, there would be no problem. There was always a bowl right beside him so he could spit whenever he needed to. We praised the effort and not the result. In fact, it was recommended that we not cheer or praise him whenever he succeeded in trying something new, as this could give him a sense of failure when he doesn't. "If my mom told me she was very proud of me when I managed to do it, I know she's disappointed with me on days I can't." But obviously on many occasions I couldn't help myself and celebrated with him, cheering and jumping for joy when he was able to overcome his fears and challenges. The first time he ate a carrot, I might as well as thrown on a carrot costume and gone parading around the neighborhood. Asking a mother not to celebrate in these circumstances is just too much. But I understood the point and almost always tried to contain myself in front of him.

All these stages of exploration could take place in the same day or evolve in stages over several of weeks. I really respected his time. If, during the first phase, just trying to get him to be near to the food, he demonstrates strong rejection, I would only work on that stage that day. If he accepted it well, then, right away, we'd move on to touch and description and so on.

We didn't follow any rules. I followed his rhythm. And every time he was in this process of having something new introduced, when he tried it, he would do an evaluation. He would write whether the food was "bad," "whatever" or "okay." Whenever we'd go back to the same food, he would evaluate it again and again... Normally we'd keep with a food for ten weeks straight.

The purpose of this technique was mainly for him to get rid of his phobia, the fear of experimenting and the aversion to certain foods, so that he, for example, would no longer have to leave the room whenever someone was eating this food. And in this process he also ended up discovering things that he could learn to like.

Like anyone else, he had a right to like or not like something—to prefer one fruit to another, one vegetable to another and so on.

After ten weeks, he would be able to either include this new food in his routine or not. For some things, he would ask that they be incorporated into the daily routine before the ten-week deadline and we'd move onto something else.

But things also went the other way. Sometimes the process was extremely arduous, involving so much suffering that he's unable to complete the full ten weeks and that was okay.

Whenever this was the case, we would take a longer break, and then, one day, later on, we'd try again. I was afraid of healing one trauma by inflicting another. I always encouraged him, but never forced him.

I think it's necessary to have respect more than anything else. And when children feel respected, they repay it in effort. And the effort is what needs to be valued and praised the most. As a mother, and as a former patient, I appreciate every achievement. For every little step, it's a big celebration. Just the fact that he tried, that he challenged himself, was already a huge victory.

I never focused on the things he still hadn't managed. I focused on how much he had successfully evolved. I never said: "But you ONLY drink two kinds of juice." When he managed to incorporate the orange juice and alternate with the lemon juice. I said, "You already drink two kinds of juice! Congratulations!" The way we say things makes a difference.

And when someone would come with a tone of criticism: "But he ONLY drinks two kinds of juice." I'd reply with a proud grin on my face: "Yes! He ALREADY drinks two kinds of juice."

As he evolved and accepted/tolerated more things, we increased the number of new foods to experiment with each week, always in the same process of exposure techniques.

I have always had a lot of patience at mealtimes and trial attempts. But I know what a lot of mothers go through and the tension that this generates in the entire family, on day trips, on vacations, in restaurants, at other people's houses—basically, in life, in general.

And it wasn't like I had patience because I'm evolved. Far from it. I'm an imperfect mother and I make lots of mistakes.

But because I had an eating disorder, I knew how he felt. I put myself in his place. I felt for him and with him. Which also had a downside. I think that, on many occasions, when he was younger, I respected him too much and, when he didn't like something, I thought with my old mindset, and I was reluctant to bring this certain thing that he had previously found repulsive, putting off introducing it into the experiment at a later date.

But I also knew, from experience, that it was no use trying to force, threaten or blackmail anyone. It might work every now and then and the child would end up eating something out of fear.

These strategies that are often used out of desperation—and I do understand that seeing your child refusing to eat can really make you desperate—aren't going to improve the child's (or adult's) relationship with food and they won't get them to create a bond of affection with food. On the contrary, with time it can get much worse.

In Theo's case, his difficulty with food was so bad that if I threatened him saying that if he didn't eat, the Bogeyman would be coming to get him, he'd ask me what time he was coming and hurry to pack his bags. He'd rather deal with the Bogeyman than the food.

Children cannot eat out of fear of threats or blackmail. They have to learn to eat out of responsibility, out of respect for their body, out of love for their body. Learning this from an early age will make all the difference throughout this child's life. Many other disorders will be avoided.

As a child, I was obligated to stay at the table until I had finished eating. I was obligated to eat things that I did not want—or rather, forced to swallow them, which is very different. Did this solve my problem? No. Did it make it worse? Maybe. Did my father do things this way because he was cruel? Definitely not. He did it out of love for me, out of desperation and because he didn't know what else to do. My parents were separated and, when I spent the holidays with my father, my breakfasts in the hotels were endless. They were battles—sources of stress that caused tension on the trip.

As a mother, I prefer to use a different strategy. Theo is very proud to be smart, so I take that route. I talk about the importance of food for the brain and what a lack of food can cause. No threats. No drama. I talk in a language that he understands and which makes him want to strive to collaborate with the treatment. Without his cooperation, there's no way to evolve. This is why I opted to play fair with him and speak openly.

The relationship of trust is something that must be preserved. I never try to trick him by putting something extra in the soup without him knowing—like throwing in a spice he doesn't like or a random a beet in the mix. First, because he'd taste it right away and, second, because I don't want to betray his trust. If I'm going to try something different, I tell him. And he might or might not want to try it.

Theo can identify things that people with ordinary palates cannot.

For example, during this treatment through the techniques of exposure, he learned to eat chicken nuggets and chicken tenders from some restaurants and fast food chains, which made our lives much easier whenever we went out to eat or travel. It was a huge win. The one he likes best is a franchise called Chick-fil-A. We usually eat or get take-out at the one in the mall. To this day, whenever I get chicken from a different Chick-fil-A location, he knows. My other son can't tell the difference and insists that it's exactly the same. Theoretically, it is the same. It's from the same restaurant chain. But he notices. And even when my husband tried to "cheat" by saying it was from the mall when it wasn't, he knew.

At first, he wouldn't eat it unless it was the "mall chicken." Nowadays, he's able to accept these variations from one place to another and he eats it without problems. He just observes where it is or isn't from, who made it or who didn't, and keeps eating.

To store his food, I use little containers that are exclusively for his meals (which have practically no seasoning). I also cook his food in a separate pot. If I prepare something in a pan that I use with the house spices, even after having thoroughly washed it and left it to soak, he can taste that the food is not the same and he's unable to eat it: "It picks up the taste."

If he gets used to drinking a specific brand of juice, he'll have enormous difficulty drinking another brand, even though it's the same flavor, and this sensitivity of liking something specific from a specific brand started back with his milk, when he was a baby. And I don't know why fate has made it this way, but much of the things he likes aren't easy to find, they're always running out, they don't have them everywhere, they stop making them, they go off the menu. It's one of life's ironic burdens.

And all of these particularities of his with eating, I know it's not just pickiness, because I'm the same way with certain things to this day. After learning about ARFID, as I mentioned in the book's introduction, I think it's very possible that I had it as a child.

You'll notice that when I wrote about the introduction of chicken nuggets and chicken fingers, I wrote "he learned to eat." When talking about the treatment of ARFID, we can't expect that the child or the adult will like something new right away. First, they learn to tolerate it. They learn that it's necessary to eat in order provide nourishment for the body, as well as because of the social matters that involve food, but the person won't necessarily eat the food because they like it.

Before his treatment, Theo used to like some things, his "safe" foods. He would eat them with pleasure, albeit in small quantities, for the reasons I mentioned. It seemed as if his body couldn't take it. And that was very difficult. Whenever he managed to introduce something new to his diet, he would take something out. To people on the outside, it might seem like compensation. "If one thing gets in, this other thing goes out." Except it wasn't... It was like he needed to make room.

So, in addition to the issue of selectivity, we had to work on the quantity, the increases.

When he managed to get used to cereal, I was really happy because this would increase his caloric intake at breakfast. But just as I was thinking that, he was telling me:

Now that I'm going to eat cereal, I can't eat bread. The first breakfast in which he managed to add a little cereal, he immediately had diarrhea. There wasn't even time to celebrate.

It wasn't behavioral. It had all this complexity of sensory difficulty and the limits of his body.

Unlike other eating disorders, he had no reference as to what normal eating was. It's not like he used to eat well and then one day he stopped eating. It's not like he compensated one food for another because he was counting calories. It's not that he liked to eat and stopped in order to lose weight. He didn't have this reference and neither did his body.

In fact, he hardly ever felt hungry. If I didn't remind him that he had to eat, he would be fine. He would "forget" to eat. There was a day when my husband and I were taking turns on an errand near our home at lunchtime, and I thought my husband had taken care of Theo's lunch and he thought I had. At 4 PM, we discovered that Theo hadn't had lunch with either one of us, and he was totally fine.

And whenever Theo conveyed to us that he was hungry (which was rare) and I thought he was going to eat a lot, instead he ate that tiny bit just as he does every day.

I'm not saying this disorder is more difficult than other eating disorders. The most difficult disorder is always going to be the one that a person has. And simply because it's their disorder. Their difficulty. Their suffering.

No one is more or less difficult. I'm merely saying that it is necessary to comprehend and understand all this complexity surrounding ARFID, so that we're able to help and respect those who have it.

PUTTING THE PUZZLE TOGETHER

FERNANDA DO VALLE

Theo was eight years old then and the treatment with exposure techniques was helping a lot with some matters, but I realized that there was still one piece of the puzzle that was missing.

The exposure helped him with the introduction of some foods, but with dairy, meat, or chicken (except in the form of ground beef and nuggets), fruits and vegetables in general, the difficulty was still enormous.

This treatment was effective in teaching him to tolerate being nearby, touching the foods in these groups I mentioned, smell their aromas, but when it came time to put them in his mouth, he might be able to do it, but the result was a very strong instant physical aversion.

He was trying really hard. How he tried! When it was time to taste the food, he would ask me to film it. Determined to succeed, he wanted to document it in order to help other children who were having the same problem. But his body reacted and prevented him from swallowing.

On the one hand, he was trying, but, on the other, a little piece of food felt like it was gigantic inside his little mouth. He would squirm, shiver, squeeze his eyes shut, contort his body, until he spit out the food or swallowed it with much difficulty.

And he felt very proud when he succeeded, but I wasn't comfortable seeing so much suffering just for him to eat a small grape, with all those physical reactions, after some 20 attempts.

I started looking for a speech therapist with experience in children's nutrition to conduct an evaluation and see if something could be done to help him with these oral issues.

When I would tell the speech therapist that he had ARFID and that I was looking for a professional that had knowledge in this area, the answer was always the same: "I don't treat such patients and I don't know anyone I might recommend."

A dear friend of mine here in the US who has a son with a speech impairment asked his speech therapist if she knew someone she could recommend. She indicated to me a center that treats eating disorders for autistic children, but which is also open to children who aren't on the spectrum.

I researched, studied and decided to make an appointment in order to better understand the line of treatment which they followed.

I spent an hour and a half with the therapist and she explained to me that their approach was based on Behavior Analysis.

As a mother, in a layperson's reading of the explanation given by the professional who attended me, I understood that this treatment would work to change his behavior toward food, with the tools to enable him to eat more functionally.

The treatment he was receiving at the time, which was based on Cognitive-Behavioral Therapy, works on the cognitive in order to change feeling, starting with thought to then reflect on behavior. But, in this new approach, he would learn to change his behavior based on interaction with the environment.

He would "learn" to eat as a responsibility, regardless of whether he enjoyed it, wanted it or liked it, minimizing his discomforts through systematic desensitization, which is a technique that gradually exposes us to the stimuli that cause our fears and phobias.

But the way she presented it to me there at this treatment center struck me as being very "mechanical."

The therapist asked me what I would do if my son wanted to go to school naked. I asked her to repeat the question, because I thought I may have misunderstood. But that's exactly what she said.

Then I answered that I wouldn't allow it and that I'd do whatever it took to get him to put on his clothes. "Naked? No way," I said. She went on, asking me what I'd do if he didn't want to do his homework.

I totally got where she was going with this. And she concluded: "Why, when it comes to food, do parents allow their children to decide whether or not they want to eat?"

I understood her point, but I don't agree that food can be viewed as a task of responsibility alone.

Of course it's necessary to develop responsibility in the act of eating for a range of reasons that I'm not going to get into now. But, I repeat, eating has all these emotional, social aspects, connections with pleasure and many other sensations that involve our affective memories.

How would he develop this emotional relationship with food if he learned to eat simply as a duty, a task to be completed, like another daily chore?

The therapist explained to me that they use a method of rewards and punishments (I wanted to use a better word here, because I find this one to be very heavy, but I couldn't find one). If the child eats a piece of food from the exposure in question, they're rewarded with something they like, like watching a video on the iPad, a scene from their favorite cartoon. If they don't eat what they're supposed to, they have to stand with their back to the wall for a certain amount of time.

I was already unsure of this method, but just imagining Theo faced with the option of standing with his back to the wall or getting a reward, Theo would choose to stand with his back to the wall without a second thought, because, for him, the worst "punishment" of all is having to eat something he couldn't stand.

Rewards never worked with him. You could offer him a trip to Disney World if he ate a banana, and surely he would choose not to take the trip, pleased with his life for having dodged that banana.

This treatment would be intensive, for three months, with a beginning, middle and end, and "enable" him to go to a classmate's party, for instance, sit and eat a piece of pizza, even without liking it, simply because everyone is eating and this is how he should behave.

I found this to be overly automated. But I didn't want to oppose it and mount a resistance before doing more research.

As they had a waiting list, I scheduled the appointment to start treatment three weeks from then and immersed myself in this universe in order to better understand it.

I began talking to some professionals in this area—some were in favor, others were completely against it. I talked with mothers who had some success with this treatment, but, after hearing about certain details, I concluded that I wouldn't be able to follow this line.

I found it very invasive and concluded that, at that moment, this treatment would not be the most appropriate for my son or myself.

I know this treatment might work for some children. There's a whole study involved, a science behind it that brings results. I know that I'm writing about isolated parts, perhaps even "text out of context," giving the impression that it is something more severe than it would be in practice, with all the techniques and trained professionals that take this approach. What's more, I'm talking about one specific location. It could well be that this technique is applied differently elsewhere.

I think that we, as mothers and fathers, have to understand our emotional limits, knowing what we can handle and what we can't. And that is one line I couldn't handle. At least at that time.

Okay, so he would eat. But at what price? How much would it cost us? How much emotional suffering would it cause in all of us as a family? Solving one problem by creating another is not something I believe to be an effective outcome. And I'm not saying that this is what would happen. Don't get me wrong. I cannot say for sure about something that I didn't experience and didn't see up close. And I really believe that the best approach is the one that works. Is it working for your child? Great! Then that's the best approach, period. If it ain't broke, don't fix it. But the way this treatment was presented to me, it didn't give me the peace of mind to give it a try.

I continued my search, looking for something that didn't just work on food. I felt that Theo needed more support.

In this investigative process, I discovered the work of the Institute of Childhood Development, conceived and coordinated by the speech therapist Dr. Patrícia Junqueira, author of the book Por que meu filho não quer comer?—Uma visão além da boca e do estômago, recommended reading for moms and dads looking for resources to help their little ones who struggle with eating challenges. Dr. Junqueira is a pioneer in Brazil in the use of a holistic approach, with an expanded vision of children with eating difficulties.

After exchanging a few emails with Dr. Junqueira, we had a long phone conversation. She explained to me how that approach works and I liked it very much. The child is evaluated as a whole and the eating difficulty is looked at like the tip of an iceberg, as a consequence of some discomfort that the child is feeling. "Not eating properly" is a response to some larger problem, which is often not visible and needs to be investigated more carefully.

Dr. Junqueira called my attention to some aspects that I had been looking at in isolation.

The whole question of sensory sensitivity that I understood as a symptom of ARFID and which I was trying to work on, in one part here, another part there, would have to be worked on together.

She suggested an assessment of his sensory processing to see if it would be appropriate to conduct a treatment that included sensory integration.

I mentioned to her that I had read a lot about Sensory Processing Disorder (SPD), and that I didn't think it fit Theo because he didn't have the behavioral issue. He doesn't display the irritability, agitation, problems socializing, problems at school. And even the whole question of his sensory sensitivity, he can adjust in most cases, except his palate. When, for example, he's bothered by brightness, he may take longer than a child who doesn't have the level of sensitivity, but he does adjust. He doesn't like noisy places, but he also adjusts. He doesn't need to flee these places, he doesn't stop playing in the sunlight, he just needs some time to regulate himself. I also stated that he had already been evaluated in the context of Autism Spectrum Disorder and did not fit the diagnosis.

Dr. Junqueira explained to me that Sensory Processing Disorder is a condition in which the individual presents difficulty processing the stimuli of the environment and the senses. And she told me that despite being confused with autism and including symptoms that are very present on the spectrum, this sensory processing flaw is a distinct disorder and can affect patients who do not have autism. She said she had seen many children with SPD that were typical, with very calm temperament, much like Theo.

I mentioned, in a previous chapter, that when I opened up about Theo's sensory sensitivity on social media, I received lots of messages from people asking me if he was autistic and many people told me that I was in denial of his "autism."

All this lack of information and the association of Sensory Processing Disorder with autism makes people think that every child who has this hypersensitivity is autistic. And in my case, even the doctors who themselves received complaints of his sensory sensitivity, having not considered him as fitting the autism scenario, did not investigate his possible sensory flaw. They just told me that with ARFID it was normal to have a sensory sensitivity, but no one suggested a holistic work.

People, whether they are laypeople or otherwise, still correlate the two diagnoses (SPD and autism), making it very difficult to seek help. I wonder how many children end up not receiving help because of this association, or how many children are not diagnosed as mildly autistic, due to this connection.

When I hung up the phone after talking with Dr. Junqueira, I was desolate. I sat in front of my house for at least an hour without reacting.

I stood there, staring at nothing, unable to process and organize the new information.

Now I was the one with the flaw in processing my thoughts and emotions.

After a while, I broke down in tears. I sobbed for at least 30 minutes, sitting in the same place.

A mixture of feelings.

First that paralyzing sense of guilt. I was struck by the desperation that came with believing that I had done everything wrong up until then. Then came the sensation of failure. And I kept asking myself: "Why didn't I connect all the dots earlier?"

It all seemed so obvious after talking to her... The missing piece of the puzzle had been found. The piece that's worth a million dollars.

But sitting there, punishing myself for something that should have been diagnosed by professionals who had all these isolated complaints right in front of them and not by me, the mother, who was not a healthcare professional, wasn't going to help Theo.

I had to remind myself that I had always done my best, with the tools and information I had available to me at the time.

I also had to keep in mind where we were when we started and how far we'd gotten. We had gained so much ground. And it hadn't been in vain. Many achievements and accomplishments should indeed be celebrated.

Now it was time to adjust the ship's sails again, to change direction—again—and push ahead in our journey.

I had to roll up my sleeves, dive headfirst into this new world and try to do damage control.

And that's exactly what I did. I did what moms always do. I got up. Mothers are like phoenixes!

Always rising from their own ashes, regenerating stronger than before!

NEW DIRECTION

FERNANDA DO VALLE

After my conversation with Dr. Patrícia Junqueira, I talked with Maria Luiza Petty, a nutritionist and one of the contributors to this book. With lots of love, affection and wisdom, she helped me find a more suitable treatment for Theo at this stage.

Malu agreed that he would benefit much more from an approach that included sensory integration, and that, in this treatment, with a broader vision, he wouldn't have to endure the suffering provoked by the other treatments, which did not consider physical limitations caused by the disorder of sensations, by the entire scenario of sensory sensitivity that he clearly presented.

I also told Malu, just as I had told Dr. Junqueira, that there was one point that still made me somewhat reluctant to agree to this new diagnostic suggestion. I mentioned to her that I did not recognize the behavioral aspect of Sensory Processing Disorder in Theo. And she told me something very interesting. Yes, it is quite common for children who have a flaw in sensory processing to present irritation, aggressiveness, agitation, anxiety and distraction as responses to this condition's symptoms. These children, who feel bothered by the stimuli that are misaligned within them, when pressured to do something for which they aren't prepared, because they haven't yet developed the necessary skills, they feel threatened, disrespected and not understood, capable of reacting and responding with unregulated behavior.

And then she told me that, because of my entire history, the experience of my eating disorder, because of my experience and understanding that his difficulty was not some kind of pickiness and because I never forced/pressured him to eat, because I never lost my patience with him in his limitations or because I never exposed him to situations of greater discomfort, he didn't develop these reactions. But the fact that he did not present these responses didn't mean that he did not have Sensory Processing Disorder.

That explanation made perfect sense to me.

Soon after that conversation, I pushed my reluctance aside and started looking for places specialized in Sensory Integration Therapy, but which also treated eating difficulties. I had read about SIT before, but because I had created this resistance due to the fact that Theo didn't present the behavioral responses and also because this condition was always associated with autism and Theo had already been assessed, I had pretty much dismissed it.

But after talking with the Dr. Junqueira and Maria Luiza, I studied the subject with an open mind and without judgment. I came to understand what sensory integration, something I had never heard of before then, was all about.

From what I read, the integration of the senses helps to organize and regulate the information on the conditions of our body and ways we respond to the environment around us based on our sensations.

When this information is in disarray, we have difficulties feeling and structuring our perception, our behavior and even our learning.

Dr. Jean Ayres, an occupational therapist who pioneered the study of Sensory Integration (SI) and began her research in the

1950s, describes SI as "the neurological process that organizes sensation from one's own body and from the environment and makes it possible to use the body effectively within the environment." (Ayres, 1989).

It is the coordination of our senses—let's pause for a sidebar here. I just recently discovered that we have more than five senses. Some approaches speak of seven, others of eight, I've read about as many as ten senses, but, here, I will consider the seven sensory systems that were mentioned by Dr. Bacy at the beginning of the book. Before we proceed, let us briefly review the sensory systems: tactile, auditory, visual, gustatory, olfactory, proprioceptive and vestibular. Five of these systems are well-known, but the less-familiar proprioceptive system is the sensory system that allows us to perceive location, the force exerted by our muscles, the position of each part of the body in relation to the others and the orientation of our body in space. And the vestibular system is formed by a set of organs of the inner ear, utilized to maintain balance, detecting important information such as gravitational changes, movement and displacement of the body.

Now, to resume... The coordination of our senses is what enables us to act and respond to situations in an appropriate way.

All this became clearer, or less complex, when I read an article from the Brazilian Association of Sensory Integration stating that, "Sensory Integration is a neurobiological process that promotes the ability to process, organize, interpret sensations and respond appropriately to the environment. It allows the senses to supply information on the physical conditions of the body and the environment and, therefore, enables the child to experience the body in everyday actions and activities. In contrast, Sensory Integration Dysfunction is a disorder in which sensory information is not properly integrated or organized in the brain. And it can produce varying degrees of problems in development, processing of information, behavior and learning—both motor and conceptual. The praxis, the ability to devise, plan and execute actions, may also be compromised. The development of the praxis is one of the objectives of Sensory Integration, which favors the practical ability to carry out the activities of daily life such as: eating, dressing, personal hygiene, playing, school activities, social participation and others. The assessment and treatment of Sensory Integration are performed by occupational therapists. The occupational therapist's general objectives are: to provide sensory experiences, assist the child in the inhibition and/or modulation of sensory information, to organize the child in the processing of the most appropriate responses to sensory stimuli, and to promote opportunities for the development of increasingly complex adaptive responses. The procedures of Sensory Integration are designed to achieve the sensory and motor foundations that help the child to learn new skills more easily. Necessarily incorporating the child's interest and motivation, the occupational therapist develops the intervention in a context of play, which involves the careful selection of sensory experiences (touch, movement, muscle and joint sensations), individually planned for each child, with challenges 'in the right proportion' to encouragement, empathy and motivation and which lead to organization (of the child and, therefore, of their nervous system)."

In addition to the articles, I also started reading books on the subject in order to have more tools to help Theo at home. I also bought books with suggestions for activities and games to help with this integration.

When I started to better understand this parallel world, which is actually not at all parallel, I was shocked at how it all began to fit together. Everything connected. It was absolutely amazing. I saw so many things in Theo once I understood this new world that had been presented to me. How important it was to learn to look "outside the box" and understand that everything was part of the same box.

In her book Everyday Games for Sensory Processing Disorder, occupational therapist Barbara Sher explains that, as with many disorders, the symptoms can occur to different degrees.

A 2009 study by the Child Mind Institute shows that one in every six children has some kind of sensory disorder that can affect learning and functioning in school. Other studies state that it is one in every 20 children. And other studies indicate that 10-15% of children suffer from Sensory Processing Disorder.

Though this disorder is very common on the autism spectrum—about 80-90% of autistic children have sensory symptoms—, it is also commonly found in children with Attention Deficit Hyperactivity Disorder (ADHD) and those with Obsessive Compulsive Disorder (OCD). And we also found this condition in children who do not have any other associated disorders.

Many professionals are still reluctant to consider this diagnosis distinctly, because, in the Diagnostic and Statistical Manual of Mental Disorders, now in its fifth edition and known as the DSM-5, Sensory Processing Disorder is only listed as a symptom under the autism scenario and not as an isolated diagnosis. But I must emphasize, yet again, that it is possible to find it in people who aren't on the spectrum. I know, I've already mentioned that. I'm being repetitive on purpose. Because this limited view on the part of healthcare professionals has delayed the search for help and a treatment that is appropriate for Theo, one that fits his needs. And the lack of information on this in our society resulted in me being harshly judged for "denying" his "autism." So I'm going to keep repeating all of this until everybody finally understands that people aren't the same as cake recipes. We are complex beings with individual needs that have to be looked at with a broader and integrated vision.

When I went to the treatment center for eating difficulties, where the approach was based on Behavior Analysis, and told them that I was opting for a treatment that included Sensory Integration Theory, because my son had Sensory Processing Disorder, and we would be freeing up Theo's spot there, the therapist told me that the choice I was making was all wrong, considering that the diagnosis was controversial, as it was not officially listed in the DSM-5. And she continued to defend her treatment's approach, criticizing my decision.

Meanwhile, in this line of treatment that I was choosing to follow, many professionals do not agree that Theo has ARFID, because they regard his difficulty with food as stemming from the sensory challenges he faces. So, according to these professionals, if it's neurological, it can't be ARFID.

Other professionals claim that he does indeed have ARFID, even with all the sensory difficulties, because this hypersensitivity is included among the symptoms of one of the condition's subtypes. But these professionals agree that he, and other children who present these sensory issues, require treatment that includes Sensory Integration therapy.

Since there's no place for profanity here, I'll behave myself. But it's not easy, as a mother, to find yourself in the middle of this struggle between approaches. Each line defends its own absolute truth—, leading you to think that what you're doing is all wrong, making you feel guiltier—, not seeking to understand that the same child can actually benefit from different, simultaneous approaches.

The exposure techniques of Cognitive-Behavioral Therapy, criticized by many professionals in the new line that I decided to follow, had benefited Theo a lot up until then. I absolutely cannot say that this approach is wrong.

In fact, to be sincere, as I've said here before and will say again, I don't believe there's a right or wrong approach. I believe in an approach that either works or does not work for each individual. All of these approaches have the same goal: to allow the child/adult to have the autonomy, ability and comfort to eat better.

Also, as a mother, whether or not he has ARFID, whether or not his Sensory Processing Disorder is part of ARFID or whether or not Theo's difficulty eating is a consequence of the flaw in his Sensory Processing simply doesn't make the slightest difference to me.

The only thing I care about is getting proper treatment to help Theo with his difficulties. I'll leave the discussion about whether the chicken or the egg came first to the professionals in each area. I just want my son to have a better quality of life, period. Regardless of the diagnosis, we all deserve to have a relationship of affection with food and our bodies.

I will get into details regarding the new approach chosen for Theo's treatment, but, first, I'd like to say that it's important to understand that we all have intolerances and sensory difficulties and we all have our own preferences, which bring us greater comfort.

To this day, I cut the labels of all my clothes because I can't stand anything chafing my skin. I've have lost count of how many pieces of clothing I ruined by cutting the fabric by accident when I cut the label off. I don't wear anything made of wool. I don't even use wool blankets (I only like cotton duvets), because it irritates me. And, for the same reason, I don't wear anything with lace either. I have problems with certain food textures and smells.

I can't get in the elevator with someone who put perfume on because it'll give me a strong headache right away. I don't like to be touched or hugged if I'm not expecting it. I feel like I'm being scratched, invaded. I don't like putting my head on anyone's lap. It's like a bed of nails to me. Holding hands? Sleeping in someone's arms? God forbids! Whoever came up with such things? I don't like people touching with my hair. I know a lot of people love getting their hair washed in the beauty salon, getting that extra little massage. I actually hate it—it hurts and I feel like running out the door.

Do I have Sensory Processing Disorder? Maybe. But I've learned to adapt and this difficulty of mine doesn't interfere with my everyday activities.

The most important factor in assessing a person is understanding the losses that this disorder brings to their life. When it starts to limit the development of a child/adult, their social interaction and daily tasks, it's time to intervene and seek help.

After understanding all this, I sought a treatment that, along with food issues, also helped Theo in the reorganization of his senses.

I found several treatment centers that are references in sensory integration here in the US. One of the most renowned is the Star Institute in Colorado. They offer various programs for eating difficulties including sensory integration.

In my research process, I attended a workshop by Dr. Kay A. Toomey PhD, a pediatric psychologist who has been working with children with feeding problems for over 30 years. She developed the SOS (Sequential Oral Sensory) approach, which is used to treat eating difficulties, integrating sensory, behavioral and nutritional factors.

And that was exactly the line adopted for food therapy at the Star Institute, which I was looking at for Theo's treatment. The first thing I did after hearing Dr. Toomey speak was get Theo a new chair. She showed us that children, especially those with sensory difficulties, need good foot support to eat. With correct posture, children feel safer and, consequently, more comfortable eating.

I found one that can be adjusted until he's tall enough that his feet touch the ground and he no longer needs the support. This chair can be used from age three on and it "grows" along with the child. If you can't afford this chair, a stool or stepladder, depending on your child's height, can be adapted to give the body this necessary support.

Unfortunately, I only learned of this detail, which made a huge difference for him, he was already eight years old. But it's never too late to change what needs to be adapted. I can't keep lamenting the things I didn't know and blaming myself (even more). Let's move forward and focus on what can be done. In the SOS Approach the goal is to increase familiarity and improve the tolerance level of food textures and smells, and thereby increase the repertoire and volume of food consumption— all through interaction and play techniques, adapted to the difficulties of each child. It uses systematic desensitization— which, as you'll recall, is a technique that gradually exposes us to the stimuli that cause us fears and phobias—to guide the child in six steps to eat. But in the SOS Approach, the technique of systematic desensitization seemed to me to be much lighter than the systematic desensitization that had been presented to me in the other treatment I was considering, based on Behavior Analysis, before finding this line that I had decided to follow from that moment on.

As the child progresses through the six steps of SOS, they learn about the sensory properties of each new food and develop oral motor skills necessary to to eat that food, reducing the stress and emotional response during meals.

In general terms, the steps are:

1. Learning to tolerate the food's presence.
2. Interacting with the food, even if just touching it through a napkin, for example. It's not necessary to have contact with the skin.
3. Learning to tolerate the smell of the food.
4. Becoming able to touch the food with your hands, without using utensils or napkins.
5. Tasting the flavor of the food without the need to chew and swallow. This could come from a little lick.
6. Successfully chewing and swallowing the proposed food, even just in small parts.

Each step still has its stages, with small goals and objectives to be achieved, and the pace will vary from child to child, always respecting the time and difficulty of each individual.

If we look at these six steps, they aren't so different from the exposure techniques of Theo's previous treatment. But the big difference is that, while these steps are worked on, in parallel, through techniques and sensory integration therapy conducted through games and in a playful manner, the child develops the skills needed to eat more comfortably. And they don't use the word "treatment." The children go to food school. Which is not the same as cooking school. He wasn't going there to learn how to cook, though some of the activities did involve cooking. But he was going to food school to overcome his difficulties in the act of eating. A school to teach him to eat better.

And they don't use the word "disorder." The term they prefer is "difficulty." So, just like when children have difficulty in mathematics, for example, they'll go to a special class to get extra help so they can do better in math, children with difficulties eating also go to a "school" to get help and learn how to eat better.

These details made a big difference to Theo. He stopped seeing himself as a having a "defect." He was able to understand more clearly, through the use of these examples, that all of us, as human beings, have our difficulties, and that's fine. This doesn't make anyone worse than anyone else. We have abilities in certain areas and difficulties in others and these differences are part of life. Difficulty is much different from disability.

This was clarified for him and he understood it easier. It was also easier for him to explain to his friends whenever they asked about his eating.

And after he began to look at all of this as difficulty, as challenges to be faced, he understood that this difficulty could be overcome. He internalized the fact that, with help, he can get better. It's no longer a label, a disease, a condition. He felt motivated to make an effort and commit himself even more. As if his energies had been recharged and his hope renewed. And mine too!

When he was about to begin the new treatment, since we were in the middle of the Covid-19 pandemic, I decided not to go to Colorado to treat Theo at the Star Institute. But I found a training center for eating difficulties called the Sensory Zone, which also included sensory integration, with the same approach as Star and with professionals who were trained by Star in Warrington, a town in the state of Pennsylvania 40 minutes from my home.

I had to wait a few weeks to be able to do Theo's sensory evaluation, because the clinic was adapting to new attendance protocols because of the pandemic.

Those weeks seemed like months. It felt like Christmas was coming, but the evaluation day would never get here. Only an anxious mom could understand what I mean.

Before the consultation, I received a number of questionnaires and forms to fill out. In the United States, it's amazing all the paperwork we have to fill out and sign for any and every little thing. Since everything has the potential to turn into a court case here, everyone tries to insulate themselves on all sides. To give you an idea: for him to do this sensory assessment, I had to sign a statement saying I was aware that he could die in treatment. Yes, you read it correctly.

But I was already used to it. When I got here five years earlier, I went to authorize my elder son to play soccer for his school, my heart almost stopped just reading the authorization clauses: "Your child can get a concussion, become paraplegic or die while playing ball…" So when It was Theo's turn, my heart had already been jaded.

This time, what most struck me was not the "risk" he was "taking," but when filling out the assessment I was shocked at how it all made sense. Before, I had only focused on taste, smell, touch, vision and hearing.

But there was much more than that. Understanding the seven senses I described earlier made me connect things that I'd never stopped to think about. All the difficulties that Theo had as a child, not only those related to food, had the same root.

The things that he had not done, which I often believed were because of laziness, were actually due to sensory difficulty. How many times had I joked with my husband that Theo was an "old soul." Before this assessment, I had never realized that his preference for more sedentary activities and that the fact that he didn't like going outside, that he didn't like riding bikes, that he wasn't able to go on the swings or the monkey bars, that he had difficulty swimming, in karate, the fact that he couldn't tie his shoelaces, and how long it took him to be able to bathe himself, to manage to squeeze the shampoo out of the container on his own, to change his clothes, to feed himself, how much he said "ow" when got his hair dried, or his hair combed, when he put on sunblock, the amount of clothing and shoes that bothered him, the difficulty he had writing, cutting with scissors and using his hands for manual activities (the period in which he did occupational therapy, described in another chapter), the way he couldn't muster the strength to open water bottles, the refrigerator and countless other things were associated with sensory difficulty.

As I answered the questions on the form, I understood that everything was part of the same package. I filled it out and cried tears by the gallon. Once again, I felt extraordinarily guilty for not having sought help earlier, for not knowing all of this when he was younger, for thinking he was lazy in some situations or fussy in others. I always understood his difficulties with food, but the other situations I didn't see as difficulties. I just hadn't had any idea. Zero understanding.

Two of the assessment's points left me simply astonished. Two things that I had complained of to the doctors, which had been investigated and nothing was found. I always heard the same thing: "It'll get better when he gets older." Except he did get older and it didn't get better.

And now, for the first time in my life, I had an explanation.

Theo took a long time to stop peeing in his sleep at night. And, even during the day, he would only run to the bathroom once he had already started going. His underwear was always wet and I asked them why he waited until the last second to go to the bathroom. He didn't know how to explain it to me properly, but he would say said that he wasn't holding it in, that he only felt the urge to go at that time. But based on the amount that he urinated, I would tell him that it was impossible that he hadn't felt it before, and asked him to pay more attention next time. How many times had I asked him if he had to pee and he'd say no, and then after we'd left the house, I'd have to pull the car over suddenly because he had started peeing his pants. And I'd say the same thing: "It's impossible that, with all this pee right now, that you didn't know you needed to pee five minutes ago." I talked to the pediatrician. We did an ultrasound of his bladder, his kidneys, and everything always normal. We had always dealt with this by taking pee "breaks," even if he didn't feel like going. And he was learning to stop everything and go to the bathroom, even when he didn't feel like he had to.

A person with Sensory Processing Disorder can have hypersensitivity, a greater sensitivity to stimuli (feeling too much) and this same child/adult may also present hyposensitivity, which is greater difficulty in processing stimuli (feeling less), for other things. In Theo's case, he had this hypersensitivity to taste, smell, touch, hearing and vision. But in terms of hunger, he had hyposensitivity. He didn't identify the signs of hunger that the rest of us normally identify. It was the same thing when it came to the urge to pee. He didn't identify the cues from his body, the warning signs. He didn't get the internal messages that it was time for him to pee. He would only feel it when he started getting wet.

And the other point of the assessment that left me dumbfounded was when I read that children with sensory difficulties can have motion sickness.

Ever since Theo was a baby, whenever he was in the car for more than 15, 20 minutes, there was a big chance he would throw up.

I used to keep those little bags you see on planes scattered in every corner, not to mention the many towels and changes of clothing that were always available to him. Once he got a little older, he learned some techniques to soothe the ill feeling, I would often spot him in the rear-view mirror taking deep breaths in a paper bag, trying to diminish the nausea. He didn't have acid reflux or any physical ailment that justified this discomfort. And it wasn't just in the car. It happened on planes, boats, amusement park rides or even activities that required him to move more.

And of course, this sick feeling that he would have in the car made him prefer to stay home and this also made him often associate eating with feeling ill. Whenever we'd go to a restaurant, for instance, he'd feel unwell on the ride home, after having eaten.

Only after we started this treatment, when he was almost nine years old did these symptoms begin to subside. Even he couldn't believe it. The first time he felt sick arriving there at the "new school," as he called the clinic, after a 40-minute drive, the occupational therapist had him lie on a large cushion and put two weighted balls on his body—treatment balls of different textures—one at his feet and the other at the height of his chest, and in a few minutes the discomfort was gone. He was so amazed by this, he told me happily, because normally whenever he had felt ill this way, it took him a long time to start feeling better again. He would get weak, pale, not have energy for anything. That same day, after I got home, I went on Amazon and bought three of these balls. The crazy mother when she stumbles onto a "miracle."

And whenever he felt this discomfort, he himself would do what he learned in the treatment with the balls. And he'd say to me, "Mom, this new school saved my life. Thanks for driving me there."

In the section of the assessment related to oral sensory processing, which is reflected in eating, I scored everything with the highest intensity. It was absolutely amazing too.

There were ten items to evaluate and I marked the maximum intensity in all but three. I answered "always" for:

- Gets anxious having certain textures of food in his mouth.
- Has an aversion to certain smells of food.
- Is unwilling to try new foods.
- Limits himself to eating a small variety of foods.
- Is selective especially in terms of textures.
- Demonstrates a strong preference for certain flavors.
- Only feels comfortable with a few foods, flavors and smells.

Another part of the assessment also really caught my attention. It was an analysis of the child's emotional response to their environment. People with Sensory Processing Disorder can have difficulties with changes in routine, environment and activities, which has always been the case with Theo. He has a hard time venturing outside of his routine, being flexible. For him, the rules are the rules and there's no way around them. And people with SPD can also have greater sensitivity in feeling, emotionally speaking.

And Theo's sensitivity wasn't just in the senses. It was always in his way of feeling emotions. Which is something wonderful. It's beautiful and touching. But he ends up suffering more in certain situations.

He's going to have to learn to pace and calibrate his emotions. If, for example, I speak to him in a more tense tone, but without getting angry, without changing the volume of my voice, he'll ask me why I'm talking to him that way. If I call his attention to something for some reason, he'll answer right away saying that he knows he's not a good son. And he's never heard anyone say anything like that at home, ever. I've never communicated such a thing to him, not in words or looks. If something happens between him and his brother, he cries and says he knows he's not a good brother.

He blames himself and even punishes himself. When he was little, he grounded himself on several occasions.

On the other hand, all this sensitivity of his makes him worry about the poor children of the world—for example, he sells lemonade (on his own initiative) to donate the money to UNICEF. He helps his friends at school. He doesn't like it when someone makes fun of someone else. If I talk about something I found funny about someone, some embarrassing situation they went through, he'll get angry: "Why did you think that was funny?" He defends his loved ones. He's extremely affectionate and observant. He likes to see people happy and to make them happy.

Theo has a wonderful heart. He's just going to have to learn to defend himself and shield himself in some situations, in order not to suffer so much. Unfortunately, real life can be cruel to those who feel things more intensely.

Please don't get me wrong. I'm not saying that everything with Theo is associated with his sensory difficulties. Not by a long shot. There is temperament, there is the environment in which he lives, reflections of his upbringing, of the mistakes we make as parents. It would be very simplistic to say that all of his physical and emotional issues are due to a flaw in his sensory processing. That would actually mean exempting myself from my responsibility as his mother to raise him. But there is a connection and I have no doubt that many things can be worked on to help him regulate his emotions and senses. The treatment alone isn't going to cure him of everything, but it will give him the tools to deal with his difficulties in a lighter way, giving him more security and providing the skills to meet the challenges.

I can't put into words how deeply moved I was by all this information that I received during his evaluation. Even with my rational side trying to remind me that I was not a professional that should have connected the dots before and that I had, on several occasions, made many isolated complaints to the pediatrician and other professionals regarding the limitations that I saw in Theo, the healthy child that he was, I was still badgering myself on how I hadn't managed to connect one thing to the other earlier. I was taken over by the same sensation I'd had when I hung up the phone with the speech therapist. Again, I was in shock. It all seemed so obvious now. Incidentally, this shocked me so because, in doing his evaluation, I identified many things in my own life, difficulties that I've always had and for which I never found an explanation. But this book isn't about me, so I'll leave my part for the next one. I just made this observation to report that my state of shock was general.

And when I received the result of the evaluation it was also very difficult to administer my emotions. All the emotions I experienced when filling out the assessment questionnaires, a mixture of anger, indignation and guilt resurged with even more intensity when I read the comments about Theo's difficulties.

In the final report, after he'd been evaluated by a team with a nutritionist, speech therapist and occupational therapist for two consecutive weeks, the following conditions were detected: low muscle tone affecting his postural stability, immature oral motor skills, sensory processing deficit interfering with his ability to perform certain tasks and attempt to try new foods, among other observations. It was eight pages long, detailing all of his sensory difficulties. After years of searching, there was finally an explanation that made sense.

I had to put my guilt aside, after all, there is no feeling that is more unproductive, that drains our energy and paralyzes us more than the guilt. Now it was up to us to focus on moving forward, on what could still be done, on being grateful for discovering all of this while he was still a child with his whole life ahead of him.

After all of these discoveries, I wanted to share with my Instagram followers, who had accompanied Theo's challenges, the new direction of his treatment. And to talk a little about the eating difficulties associated with Sensory Processing Disorder, I invited Carla Deliberato, owner of the Maternal and Childcare Clinic in São Paulo, a speech therapist with vast experience in childhood food refusal and selectivity. I met her during my research process described in the chapter "Putting the puzzle together." At that time, I exchanged messages with Carla. She was extremely caring and welcoming. She even recommended a fantastic book that would prove to be a huge help, Food Chaining: The Proven 6-Step Plan to Stop Picky Eating, Solve Feeding Problems and Expand Your Child's Diet. She is one of the few professionals in Brazil who has a more comprehensive and cohesive vision of food difficulties. One thing that really surprised me was that, before the live stream that I scheduled with Carla, I posted a survey on my profile, asking who had ever heard of SPD. To my surprise, only 6% of my audience, which is composed of lots of healthcare professionals, knew about Sensory Processing Disorder. Well, I think this clearly shows that we need to talk about it more.

When Theo started the new treatment here in the US, he would go to his "new school" twice a week for an hour and a half each day. He would spend 45 minutes in the sensory integration room with an occupational therapist and then another 45 minutes with the food therapist doing the taste trial. The taste trial is nothing more than the exposure technique, but with a few modifications. The team investigates according to what the child already eats and, from there, everything is done adapting the food to a texture that the child is likely to tolerate.

So, for example, when Theo began with this approach, he was unable to eat bananas, because the texture would cause him anxiety, even though he liked the taste. To introduce this fruit to his diet, the team charted what he was able to eat at that time. They concluded that the best way to introduce the banana would be in pancake batter, because the texture of the pancake was closer to the foods he ate without difficulty. If, by chance, it was easier for him to accept crispy textures, they would have incorporated the banana into a more solid recipe, perhaps a cookie, and so on.

In parallel to the steps of the taste trial, he worked on developing his oral motor skills through techniques and exercises to enable him to accept new textures with comfort. The greater the comfort, the less the resistance.

Even there in the treatment, he wasn't obliged to try anything, and anything he put in his mouth, he could spit out, without no pressure or expectations.

I always sent in something that he already ate, something he tolerated and something new. And he would evaluate these foods every week. The process was very similar to the previous one, but in a lighter and more playful way and respecting the comfort of the textures that provided him with security.

At home, we also made some modifications according to the team's guidelines. We started having family style meals. He was no longer given his food already on the plate. Everything came to be part of the meal, even though he knew only he would eat the bean soup. Everything was served in bowls at the center of the table and rather than Theo's menu be soup and the rest of the family's be x, y or z, there was one single menu—as in, "Today, we're having bean soup, chicken breast, vegetable risotto and salad." He even started serving himself and we would pass the bowls around so everyone could serve themselves what they wanted. Next to his plate, I'd put two pots, which we called pots of experimentation. If he wanted to, he could put something there that was on the table to try or just keep it near him. It was a way for him to avoid feeling pressured to put something on the plate he was eating from, to have something touch his food or even think that if he put it on the plate, he'd have to eat it. And the rule was the same: if he tried it and didn't like it, he could spit it out. And no one could judge him or insist. Incidentally, the guidelines were for us to talk about everything at the table except food.

The lightness of mealtime started to make him feel more comfortable, more relaxed, and he became more curious about the food. He started asking about what we were eating, what it felt like in our mouths, how it was made, things for which he showed no previous interest.

I remember that, two weeks after the treatment, one day he came into the kitchen and said to me: "Hey Mom, where's my lunch? I'm starving!"

"Just a minute, son... Excuse me while I pass from emotion. I'll be right back." That's what I wanted to say, but I acted naturally, telling him that lunch was almost ready. As soon as he was out of earshot, I cried wholeheartedly, jumped up and thanked God, the Universe and all the saints whose names I could remember. I even thanked Our Lady of Food!

Theo didn't eat too much that day. It was the same little bit he had every day, but the fact that he could recognize the signal of hunger in the body was something to be celebrated. It had been eight years of him scarcely ever saying he was hungry, and whenever I asked, the answer was always no. These are details that might seem subtle, but which are huge advances: him learning to understand and trust his own body.

And I stopped asking him to try "just one more spoonful," after he'd said he was full. The first few times were very difficult for me, because I thought: "But he would always eat one more spoonful whenever I said that. This spoonful will be missed." And after a few days, whenever he said he was full, I would keep eating my food, not saying anything, not asking him to have another spoonful. He pushed his plate away and stayed there at the table. Then, suddenly, he'd pull his plate back and say, "I think I'm going to eat a little more." And not only did he eat the "extra" spoonful I normally asked him to eat, but he'd two or three more and sometimes even finish the dish. The tears started flowing and I had to pretend I was sneezing, saying I was having a sinus attack, to disguise the emotions I felt seeing him succeed.

Another change at home was to start spacing out the days when Theo would have his favorite foods so as to avoid what they call food jag—when the child only eats the same food, prepared in exactly the same way, day after day, sometimes meal after meal, and from eating the same thing so often the child gets sick of it and eliminates this food from their diet, not being able to stand the sight of it anymore, making them more selective and restrictive, because you can't always introduce something new in its place. So that oatmeal cookie that he used to eat every day, he started having every other day. And this made it much easier to vary the menu more. Of course, everything was agreed upon with him. We would sit down together and, in order to keep him from getting anxious not knowing what would be available that day, devise the menu for that week together. Obviously, there could be some flexibility, but having that routine helped him a lot.

And getting him to participate in the decisions, the choices, made him feel in control.

All these changes were reflected in the day-to-day and he was feeling increasingly secure trying new foods and having new foods introduce to the menu.

We did some activities at home to complement the treatment, always at the suggestion of the team, with the aim of reinforcing what was being worked on that week at "school."

One simple, playful activity that was very important for Theo was "drawing" and "writing" with food. With it, he confronted numerous challenges at the same time:

- being close to foods that were challenging to him,
- tolerating the smell
- and touching and exploring new textures.

He even worked on his fine motor coordination in these dynamics. When we used peas or corn, for example, he made a pinching movement with his fingers, helping him to have better motor skills. And this simple activity also stimulated him in creativity, and in planning, and it has helped him concentrate and focus on the execution of ideas, very important steps when working on sensory integration.

Another thing that helped Theo a lot was a conversation he had with his dentist at one of the routine consultations, around the time he was beginning the new treatment. The day before this consultation, I talked to the dentist on the phone and told him about Theo's fear of breaking a tooth when eating harder foods, as well as his current treatment. I talked about the new discoveries regarding the sensory issues and how this was reflected even in the act of brushing his teeth, because, since he experienced discomfort in his mouth, he had difficulty brushing more deeply, and that there was not an explanation to him saying "ouch, ouch" when he brushed.

The dentist was great with Theo and came up with something that made a huge difference for my little guy. He not only explained how resistant our teeth are, giving him examples, but he also talked about the importance of some foods that Theo was afraid to eat for healthy teeth. He showed how a raw carrot has the function of "self-cleaning" our teeth, the extent to which it helps prevent the accumulation of tartar. He gave him some exercises to do at home, initially with apples and carrots, so he could build his confidence and see that his teeth are stronger than he thought. This experience made Theo see food in a broader way... a vision that goes beyond eating: the benefits, the different functions, all complementing one another.

Food therapy, along with sensory integration, also helped him with his independence, his power to decide—he started to decide between wanting or not wanting... His choices were no longer limited by whether or not he was able. He came to have autonomy. He learned to listen to his body and his urges.

He began to understand what was happening to him and why he was "different" from his friends in certain aspects. We also started look at him differently. Before, we thought he had a quieter, more resigned temperament, that he was less active. And we respected that. I never thought that he didn't do certain things because he didn't have the ability to complete given activities. I thought it was because he simply didn't like them. And, as he was feeling more comfortable in his own body and his abilities improved, he became fond of doing things he didn't think he would like. We started stimulating him, but in the correct way. Without pressuring him, without thinking he was "lazy" and giving him the resources, he needed to do it. And with all this "mixed together," starting to eat better and losing the fear of trying new foods, Theo came to be sure of himself.

He started laughing more and demanding less of himself. He started having more fun, including with food. We went to the kitchen more to test new recipes. We talked about everything and the subject of food was no longer a boogeyman.

Life got less tense. The mood at home became lighter, with meals in harmony.

We started to create memories at the dinner table.

He became more willing to play, to go outside and to simply BE A KID.

STIGMA

FERNANDA DO VALLE

I commented a little in the introduction to this book that I had already a few hard truths, or rather many "half-truths," in relation to the feeding of my son.

Before he got the diagnosis, I found myself often being judged, including by people close to me.

I thought that after I explained his diagnosis, people would understand.

Some did, others still didn't. They just didn't want to learn.

I concluded that, with or without the diagnosis, some people simply don't want to understand that this is a feeding difficulty, and that it's not Theo's fault, not mine or anyone else's.

I thought that, by bringing the information, people would be more empathetic and accepting.

Here, in the United States, I feel much more welcomed, not only by health professionals, but also by laypeople. People say that Americans are cold. It just depends on you mean by "cold."

They don't take to hugging, kissing, physical contact. Parties, even for adults, have a scheduled time to start and end. Americans aren't ones to meddle in other people's business, or show up at your house unannounced. Believe me, this is not my idea of coldness; it's actually a dream come true.

Culturally, Americans have an admirable ability to put themselves in the shoes of others and a much greater sense of community than Brazilians do. I've learned a lot in my years living here.

"It takes a village to raise child," is an African proverb that people often use in the United States, which speaks of the community's importance in the lives of families.

When I decided to open up about Theo's ARFID in my social media, with the intention of helping other families and people who go through this, I received hundreds of messages of people who don't even knew me, judging me with hostility and aggressiveness. In addition to the judgment that I recounted in a previous chapter, on the question of him being autistic, a lot of people told me that if he were poor he wouldn't have "this ARFID thing" and that it's a rich people illness– as if eating disorders chose people based on purchasing power and social class.

One message told me that it was because I "didn't use the belt." It's so sad to think that there are people who believe this problem can be solved by hitting.

It made me imagine how many children out there get beatings to make them eat their food. My heart aches just at the thought of violence, even verbal violence, against a child (and adults too).

Another person told me that I should stop the treatment, because he would end up "getting hooked on" eating and not be able to stop. This human being, or rather inhumane being, claimed that Theo was going to get fat and I was going to regret having "insisted" that eat.

Some of the messages told me: "Send him to my house. I guarantee you he'll eat."

How so? What could this person be thinking? That there's no food in my house?

When I started exposing Theo's treatment, through videos (with his knowledge and consent) that showed his difficulties and advances, rather than focusing on the evolution of the treatment, people preferred to opine about the choice of food, the method of preparation and would even say things like: "But raw carrots won't do. I'll send you some recipes."

And with all the patience in the world, holding back the urge to unleash a barrage of profanity, I explained that it wasn't a question of seasoning (because he never liked seasoning and the blander the food the easier, or, rather, the less difficult), but instead for him to become accustomed to the texture, the smell... and that he preferred to eat that way... and blah-blah-blah.

The messages were harsh and cruel. I was sentenced. Judged and convicted.

The only reason I didn't give up exposing my son's case was because, in the same proportion that I received these offensive messages, I also received hundreds of messages from people thanking me for talking about this subject.

There were countless messages from mothers, with moving expressions of gratitude.

Let me transcribe a message here that really touched me:

Good evening, Fernanda,

Tonight was a breakthrough night. My sister-in-law sent me the link of your live stream with Dr. Bacy. It made my heart race. You have no idea of the good you're doing for thousands of mothers who are watching you. Pay no attention to the criticism of your child. You're giving yourself to a greater mission.

My son has ARFID. He was diagnosed two years ago. Today he's 16, but the problem began at age two.

In your live stream, you and Dr. Bacy described our entire lives. I saw a movie playing in my mind. My child has the three ARFID subtypes. We went through dozens of pediatricians, psychologists, psychiatrists and neurologists, and no one was able to diagnose it.

We were fortunate to find a psychologist who did diagnose it. He's in therapy with her, but unfortunately, we live in rural Minas Gerais and we don't have psychiatrists that specialize in ARFID here.

The psychiatrists who treated him came up with various misdiagnoses. The last one said he had ADHD. Please...

Today he eats only 25 types of food and receives treatment from an endocrine/clinical nutritionist.

This is how he survives. He is short in stature and low in weight. I was already quite discouraged to keep looking for psychiatrists, because over the years we haven't gotten any palpable result. But today you have brought hope to our hearts. My husband and I watched your live stream with a twinkle in our eyes. I want to express my great thanks.

Stay firm in your purpose, because you have no idea the extent of your mission.

Warm regards,
Márcia Jones

So even as some people continued to throw stones, I persisted on my path and kept talking about this subject. For Marcia Jones and so many other mothers here, represented by her. Children with feeding difficulties started watching Theo's videos and began to feel welcomed and relieved knowing that other children were going through the same thing they were. I got a video from a boy who asked his mother to record him trying a new food, after not having tried anything new for a long time, wanting to show Theo that he could do it, too.

It was one of the most touching moments I've experienced since I started talking about ARFID.

And I also went ahead to show that, in addition to the fact that ARFID is not pickiness, recovery doesn't depend only on the wishes of the family and the child or adult. Awareness alone doesn't generate change.

Many times, Theo wanted, he tried, he fought, but the symptoms were stronger than he was. And for this reason it is extremely important to seek help and follow a treatment, with an interdisciplinary team, with professionals specialized in eating disorders.

Getting treatment from a professional who is unaware of ARFID, in addition to not providing help, can actually make the condition worse.

Unfortunately, along this path, I met dozens of people who are now adults and, due to lack of treatment in childhood, have chronic ARFID and suffered irreversible harm. Even today, following an appropriate treatment, the difficulty in reversing this situation is much greater.

The sooner you get treatment, the higher the quality of (physical and emotional) life this child will have as they grow into adulthood and the greater the expectation for a cure.

The good news of this book isn't that Theo has been completely cured. And my hope for a cure isn't that he'll eat any and everything. We can all have our personal preferences and that's fine.

This book closes with him eating more food options than he did before the treatment.

A few months ago he would only drink lemonade, one specific brand of lemonade and in just one type of cup. Today he drinks other brands of lemonade, in different cups or straight from the bottle. He also drinks orange, grape and apple juice. Often, we tend to always look at what's missing or what has not yet worked and here many people might think: "But what about the juices made from other fruits?"

Calm down, people! It's a process, not a miracle. And to be perfectly honest, he's doing great. I'm incredibly happy with him drinking these flavors of juice. For me and for him, four flavors of juice is something sensational. It is the realization that it is possible to change and to improve. It means overcoming. It means celebration! With a little dance of joy and everything!

I end this book with him telling me that he's hungry, knowing how to identify this important internal signal of his body. (Ah! How I'm beaming, my little one!).

I finish this work seeing him with more than one food on his plate. With him eating rice and beef, without fear of one food touching the other. And with him expressing a desire to eat some things.

"Hey, where are the vegetables? Where's the colorful dish?"

We'll get there. I'm sure of it. But without skipping steps, without pressure, with plenty of love, affection, patience and dedication.

We've already made it to some fruits, a cheese, a carrot, a steak, new snacks. Isn't it wonderful?

Today he has more curiosity and less anxiety. He knows what a craving is. He knows what it means to be full. And this is victory!!

I know that some people will still tell me that he eats such a small variety and a small amount compared to other children. And I think it's all a matter of reference. I only compare him to himself. Where he was and where he is now. And here, let me leave my wishes for my son documented:

My little giant Theo,

First of all, I want to tell you how proud I am of your strength, your determination, your achievements, breakthroughs and victories. I wish you more and more comfort and more pleasure in eating. That you'll be able to eat enough – in quantity and in variety – to obtain, from food, the nutrients you need to grow and develop, without needing supplementation from vitamins.

I hope you'll be able to eat in social situations, without it being stressful or uncomfortable, and without having to disguise or justify yourself whenever something is offered to you.

I want you to have the confidence to decide whether or not you want to eat something, for yourself, for your own volition and satisfaction, and not out of fear, pressure or tension.

And above all, my son, that you're able to, create emotional memories through food and the moments that involve eating with family and friends, because I believe very strongly that food is affection.

And I wish from the bottom of my heart that you're able to love and feel loved at many dinner tables.

With love,
Mommy

He has not yet achieved all of these goals, but he has already evolved A LOT and he's on his way.

I couldn't wait for all this to happen to write this book, as people urgently need more information.

Families need support. They need understanding and empathy. They need to be embraced, cared for and welcomed. And not judged.

And I have no doubt that I will soon write another book telling you more about my son's achievements. I also want to write more about Sensory Processing Disorder and all the new discoveries that I've made.

But the good news of this book is that I 've found my north star. And, just as I wrote in the introduction, the four of us, three professionals and one mother, came together to show you that there is a light, there are paths and there are treatments.

And we're not here to force any path on you. We're not here to tell you what treatment you must choose to follow.

I particularly do not believe in absolute truth.

In fact, be wary of any professionals who thump their chest and insist they're right and the world is wrong.

I do not believe that there is just one approach that works and that all others are no good. As I said in the previous chapter, I do not believe that there is the right approach and the wrong treatment. I believe strongly in what does and doesn't work for a child, for an individual.

I didn't get Theo's treatment right the first time. I went through a lot, bumped my head along the way and might still stumble on this journey.

And just like me, you as a mother or father will have the sensitivity to choose the best for your child.

Follow your heart. Listen to your intuition.

And don't give up searching and fighting. You will find the cure!

We're all in this together. Warmly,
Fernanda do Valle

SPECIAL THANKS

FERNANDA DO VALLE

    To those who believed in this project and helped me make it possible: my eternal editor Antonio Simplicio and Herbert Junior, my partner designer in all my works. To my companions in studies and research, Bacy, Manu and Malu, thank you for accepting this invitation and for all the affection and dedication to make this dream a reality.

    To my family for all the support always: Vicente, my companion on this journey, thank you for all the support and for always encouraging my work. To my sons Theo and Daniel, thank you for awakening in me the desire to want to be a better person. To my stepdaughters Thata and Kakau, thank you for all the support always. To my crooked son, Hugão, I love you very much. To my mother, thank you for always applauding me and not allowing me to quit. To my sisters, Pat and Lelê, thank you for always being on my side. To my brother Lorenzo, you're the gift Daddy gave me. And to Papito, thank you for leaving me a little bit of your gift for communication.

    To my sisters Dani and Lu, from the bottom of my heart for all the love, friendship and help as always. Thank you for your patience and excellence in revising my texts. And thank you for introducing me to ARFID.

    I would like to thank a dear friend that ARFID gave me. Carol, thank you for so many wonderful exchanges. Thanks for all the material you shared. Thank you for providing me with so much information and especially for sharing with me what you have that is most precious, your David.

And I thank all the mothers who embraced me and shared with me their stories, their victories, their pains, their fears and yearnings.

Now we're all in this together. No one let go of anyone else's hand.

DR. BACY FLEITLICH-BILYK

To my children Ana and Tiago, with my (truly!) unconditional love.

To Paulo Bilyk, who gave me my two loves and who always believed, supported and motivated my career.

Also with great respect and deep admiration to the two great masters who inspired me and guided my entire professional career: Professor Valentim Gentil and Professor Robert Goodman.

To all of you, thank you so much!

MANOELA FIGUEIREDO

To my son Antonio, who as a baby gave a little work getting him to eat, but who today is an intuitive eater with gusto. To my partners at Genta and all my colleagues who study and work with eating disorders and help their patients in search of a better relationship with food.

MARIA LUIZA PETTY

To my family for the opportunity to study and work with something that, in addition to giving me satisfaction, is able to help those who need it. To my colleagues at Ambulim and Genta for teaching me, inspiring me and accompanying me on a more human nutrition.

REFERENCES

ADDESSI, E; GALLOWAY, AT; VISALBERGHI, E; BIRCH, LL. Specific social influences on the acceptance of novel foods in 2-5-year-old children. Appetite. 2005; 45 (3):264-271.
APA – AMERICAN PSYCHIATRIC ASSOCIATION. Diagnostic and Statistical Manual of Mental Disorders (DSM-5): 5th ed. Washington, DC, USA: American Psychiatric Publishing; 2013.

AYRES, AJ. What's Sensory Integration? An Introduction to the Concept. In: Sensory Integration and the Child: 25th Anniversary Edition. Los Angeles: Western Psychological Services, 2005.
BATSELL, RW; BROWN, AS; ANSFIELD, ME; PASCHALL, GY. You Will Eat All Of That!: a Retrospective Analysis of Forced Consumption Episodes. Appetite. 2002; 38(3): 211–219.

BIEL, L; PESKE, N. Raising a Sensory Smart Child: The Definitive Handbook for Helping Your Child with Sensory Processing Issues: 3rd ed. New York: Penguin Books, 2018.
BIRCH, LL; DOUB, AE. Learning to Eat: Birth to Age 2 y. Am J Clin Nutr. 2014; 99 (3):723S-728S.

BRYANT-WAUGH, R. ARFID – Avoidant Restrictive Food Intake Disorder: A Guide for Parents and Carers: 1st ed. New York: Routledge, 2020.

BRYANT-WAUGH, R. Overview of the Eating Disorders. In: Bryant- Waugh R, Lask B, editors. Anorexia Nervosa and Related

Eating Disorders in Childhood and Adolescence, 2nd ed. London: Psychology Press, 1999.

CARRUTH, BR; ZIEGLER, PJ; GORDON, A; BARR, SI. Prevalence of Picky Eaters among Infants and Toddlers and Their Caregivers' Decisions about Offering a New Food. J Am Diet Assoc. 2004; 104 (1 suppl 1):57–64.

CHATOOR, I. Feeding Disorders in Infants and Toddlers: Diagnosis and Treatment. Child Adolesc Psychiatr Clin N Am. 2002; 11(2):163-183. COOKE, L. The Importance of Exposure for Healthy Eating in Child- hood: a Review. J Hum Nutr Diet. 2007a; 20(4):294-301.

DOVEY, TM; STAPLES, PA; GIBSON, EL; HALFORD, JC. Food Neophobia and 'Picky/Fussy' Eating in Children: a Review. Appetite. 2008; 50(2-3):181-193. FARROW, CV; COULTHARD, H. Relationships between Sensory Sensitivity, Anxiety and Selective Eating in Children. Appetite. 2012;58(3):842-6.

FRAKER, C; FISHBEIN, M; COX, S; WALBERT, L. Food Chaining: The Proven 6-Step Plan to Stop Picky Eating, Solve Feeding Problems, and Expand Your Child's Diet. Cambridge,: Da Capo Press, 2007.

GALLOWAY, AT; FIORITO, L; LEE, Y; BIRCH, LL. Parental Pressure, DietaryPatterns, and Weight Status among Girls Who are "Picky Eaters". J Am Diet Assoc. 2005; 105 (4):541-548. GALLOWAY, AT; FIORITO, LM; LEE, Y; FRANCIS, LA; BIRCH, LL. 'Finish Your Soup': Counterproductive Effects of Pressuring Children to Eat on Intake and Affect. Appetite. 2006; 46: 318–323.

GALLOWAY, AT; LEE, Y; BIRCH, LL. Predictors and Consequences of Food Neophobia and Pickiness in Young Girls. J Am Diet Assoc. 2003; 103(6):692-698.

HARRIS, G; SHEA, E. Food Refusal and Avoidant Eating in Children: including those with Autism Spectrum Conditions. A Practical Guide for Parents and Professionals: 1st ed. London: Jessica Kingsley Publishers, 2018.

HENDY, HM; WILLIAMS, KE; RIEGEL, K; PAUL, C. Parent Mealtime Actions that Mediate Associations between Children's Fussy-eating and Their Weight and Diet. Appetite. 2010; 54 (1): 191-195.

JACOBI, C; AGRAS, WS; BRYSON, S; HAMMER, LD. Behavioral Validation, Precursors, and Concomitants of Picky Eating in Childhood. J Am Acad Child Adolesc Psychiatry. 2003; 42(1):76-84.

JUNQUEIRA, P. Por que meu filho não quer comer? Uma visão além da boca e do estômago. Bauru: Ideia Editora, 2017.

KATJA, R; MCGLTHLIN, J. Helping your Child with Extreme Picky Eating. Oakland: New Harbinger Publications, Inc; 2015.
KERZNER, B; MILANO, K; MACLEAN, WC JR; BERALL, G; STU- ART, S; CHATOOR, I. A Practical Approach to Classifying and Managing Feeding Difficulties. Pediatrics. 2015; 135 (2):344-353.

KLEIN, M. Anxious Eaters, Anxious Mealtimes: Practical and Com- passionate Strategies for Mealtime Peace. Bloomington: Archway Publishing, 2019.
LASK, B; BRYANT-WAUCH, R. Childhood Onset Anorexia Nervosa and Related Eating Disorders. East Sussex: Psychology Press, 1996.

MICALI, N; SIMONOFF, E; ELBERLING, H; RASK, CU; OLSEN, EM; SKOVGAARD, AM. Eating Patterns in a Population-based Sample of Children Aged 5 to 7 Years: Association with Psychopathology and Parentally Perceived Impairment. J Dev Behav Pediatr. 2011; 32:572–580.

NEDA Feeding Hope (Online) www.nationaleatingdisorders.org/arfid

NEWMAN, J; TAYLOR, A. Effect of a Means-end Contingency on Young Children's Food Preferences. J Exp Child Psychol. 1992; 55: 431-439.
ORRELL-VALENTE, JK; HILL, LG; BRECHWALD, WA; DODGE, KA; PETTIT, GS; BATES, JE. "Just Three More Bites": an Observational Analysis of Parents' Socialization of Children's Eating at Mealtime. Appetite. 2007;48(1):37-45.

PEARSON, N; BIDDLE, SJH; GORELY, T. Family Correlates of Fruit and Vegetable Consumption in Children and Adolescents: a Systematic Review. Public Health Nutr. 2008; 12(2): 267–283.
PETTY, MLB. Comportamentos dos pais em relação à alimentação dos filhos e comportamentos alimentares de crianças com dificuldades alimentares, obesas e eutróficas. Tese (Doutorado em Ciências) – Universidade Federal de São Paulo, São Paulo.

_____. Dificuldades alimentares na infância e transtorno alimentar restritivo evitativo. In: Transtornos Alimentares e Nutrição: da prevenção ao tratamento. Barueri: Manole, 2020. P. 39 – 66.

_____; FIGUEIREDO, M; KORITAR, P; DERAM, S; PASCOAL, C. Nutrição comportamental no atendimento de crianças e adolescentes. In: Alvarenga, M; Figueiredo, M; Timerman, F. Nutrição comporta- mental. 2. ed. Barueri: Manole, 2019. p. 433-63.

ROWELL, K; McGLOTHLIN, J. Helping Your Child with Extreme Picky Eating: A Step-by-Step Guide for Overcoming Selective Eating, Food Aversion, and Feeding Disorders. Oakland: New Harbinger Publications, Inc, 2015.

SATTER, E. Feeding Dynamics: Helping Children to Eat Well. J Pediatr Health Care. 1995;9(4):178-84.
SHIM, JE; KIM, J; MATHAI, RA; STRONG Kids Research Team. Associations of Infant Feeding Practices and Picky Eating Behaviors of Preschool Children. J Am Diet Assoc. 2011;111(9):1363-1368.

SMITH, AM; ROUX, S; NAIDOO, NT; VENTER, DJ. Food Choice of Tactile Defensive Children. Nutrition. 2005; 21 (1):14-19. STEINSBEKK, S; BONNEVILLE-ROUSSY, A; FILDES, A; LLEWELLYN, CH; WICHSTROM, L. Child and Parent Predictors of Picky Eating from Preschool to School Age. Int J Behav Nutr Phys Act. 2017;14(1):87.

THOMAS, J; EDDY, K. Cognitive-Behavioral Therapy for Avoidant/ Restrictive Food Intake Disorder. Cambridge: Cambridge University Press, 2019. THOMAS, JJ; LAWSON, EA; MICALI, N; MISRA, M; DECKERSBACH, T; EDDY, KT. Avoidant/Restrictive Food Intake Disorder: A Three Dimensional Model of Neurobiology with Implications for Etiology and Treatment. Curr Psychiatry Rep.2017;19 (8):54.

TOOMEY, K. Picky Eaters vs Problem Feeders/SOS Approach to Feeding. (Online) Sosapproachconferences.com. US National Library of Medicine National Institutes of Health. (Online) ncbi.nlm.nih.gov.

VAN DER HORST, K; DEMING, DM; LESNIAUSKAS, R; CARR, BT; REIDY, KC. Picky Eating: Associations with Child Eating Characteristics and Food Intake. Appetite. 2016;103: 286-93. VAN TINE, ML; MCNICHOLAS, F; SAFER, DL; AGRAS, WS. Follow-up of Selective Eaters from Childhood to Adulthood. Eat Behav. 2017; 26:61-65.

WILLIAMS, KE; FIELD, DG; SEIVERLING, L. Food Refusal in Children: a Review of the Literature. Res Dev Disabil. 2010; 31 (3):625-633.

Made in the USA
Monee, IL
10 February 2024